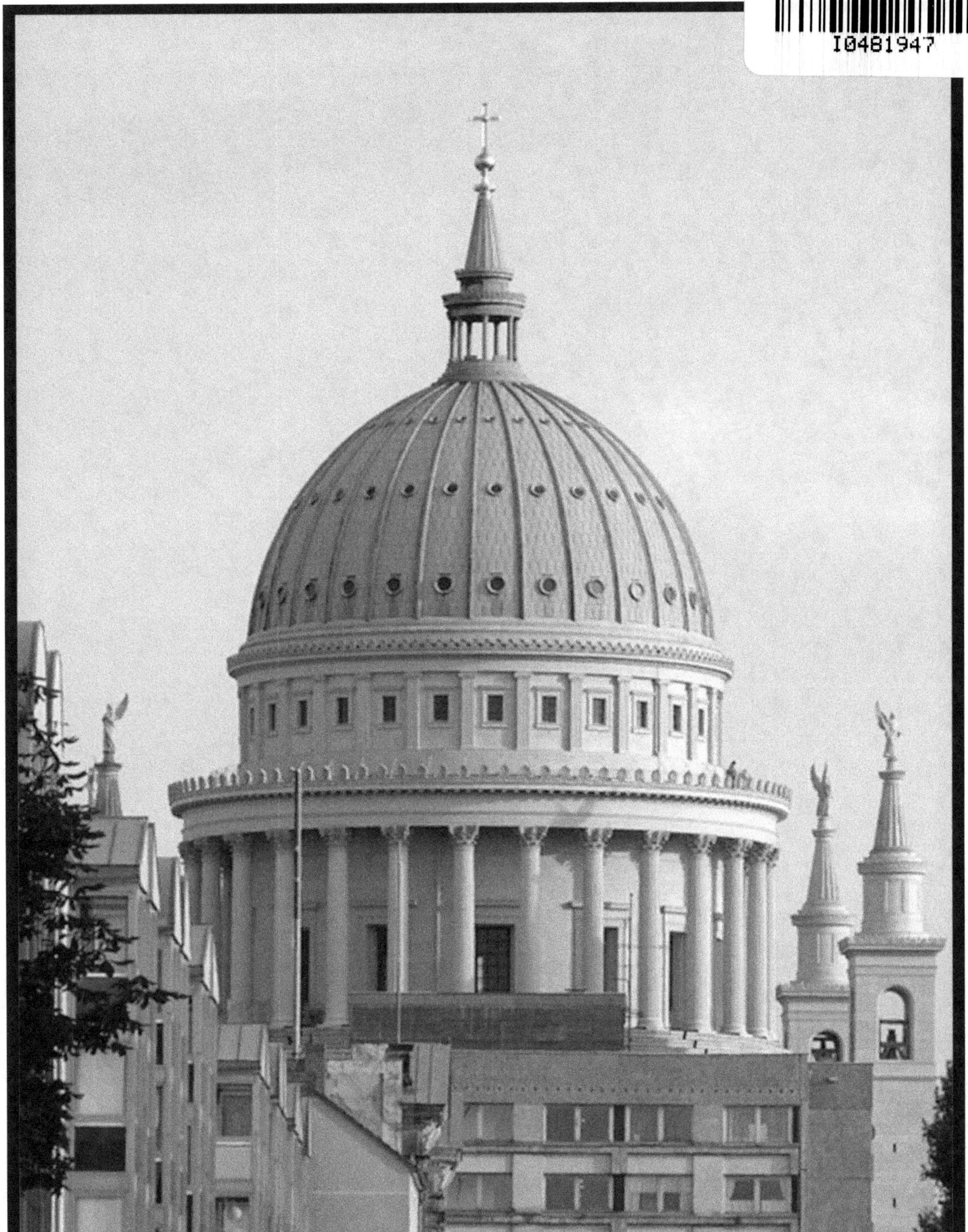

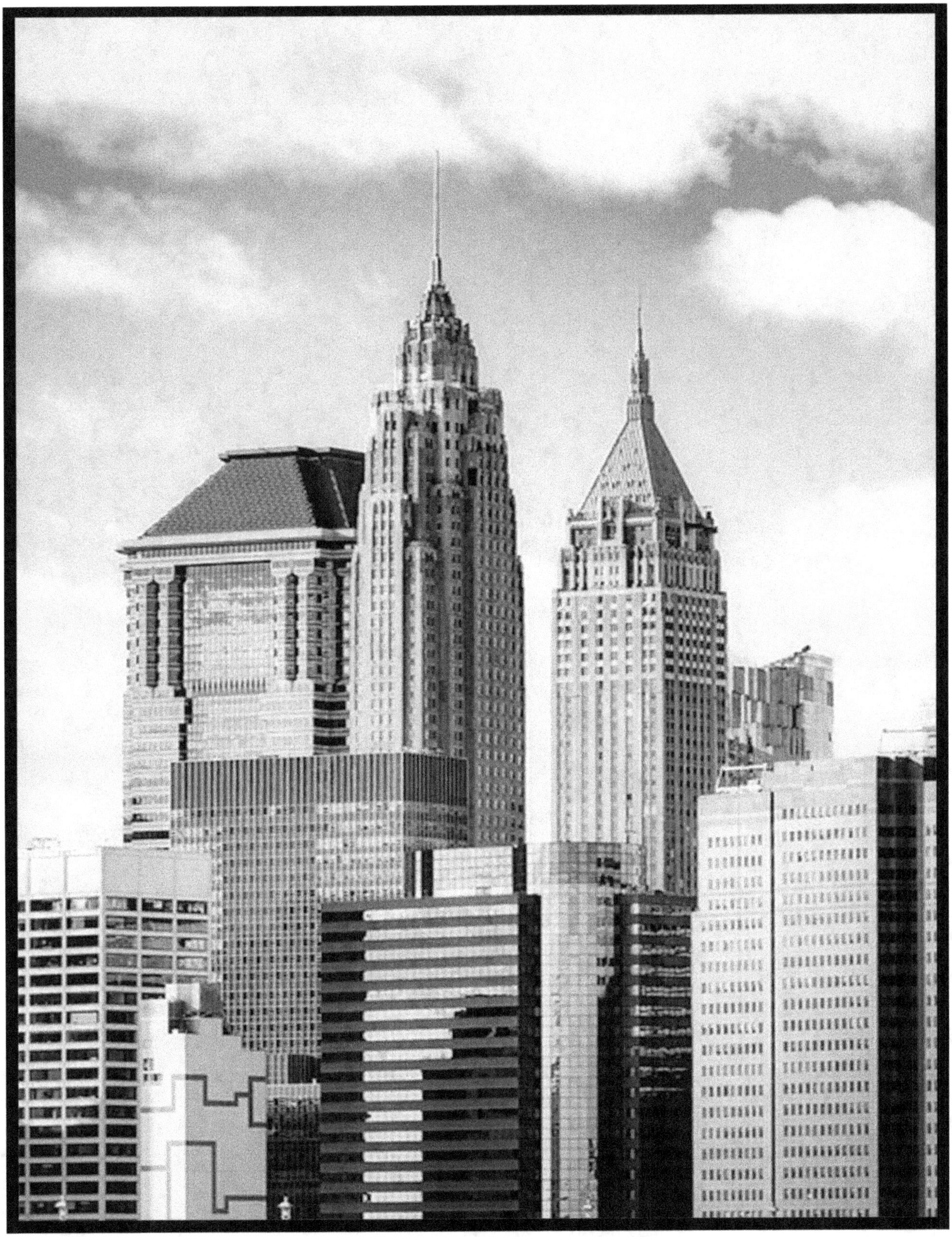

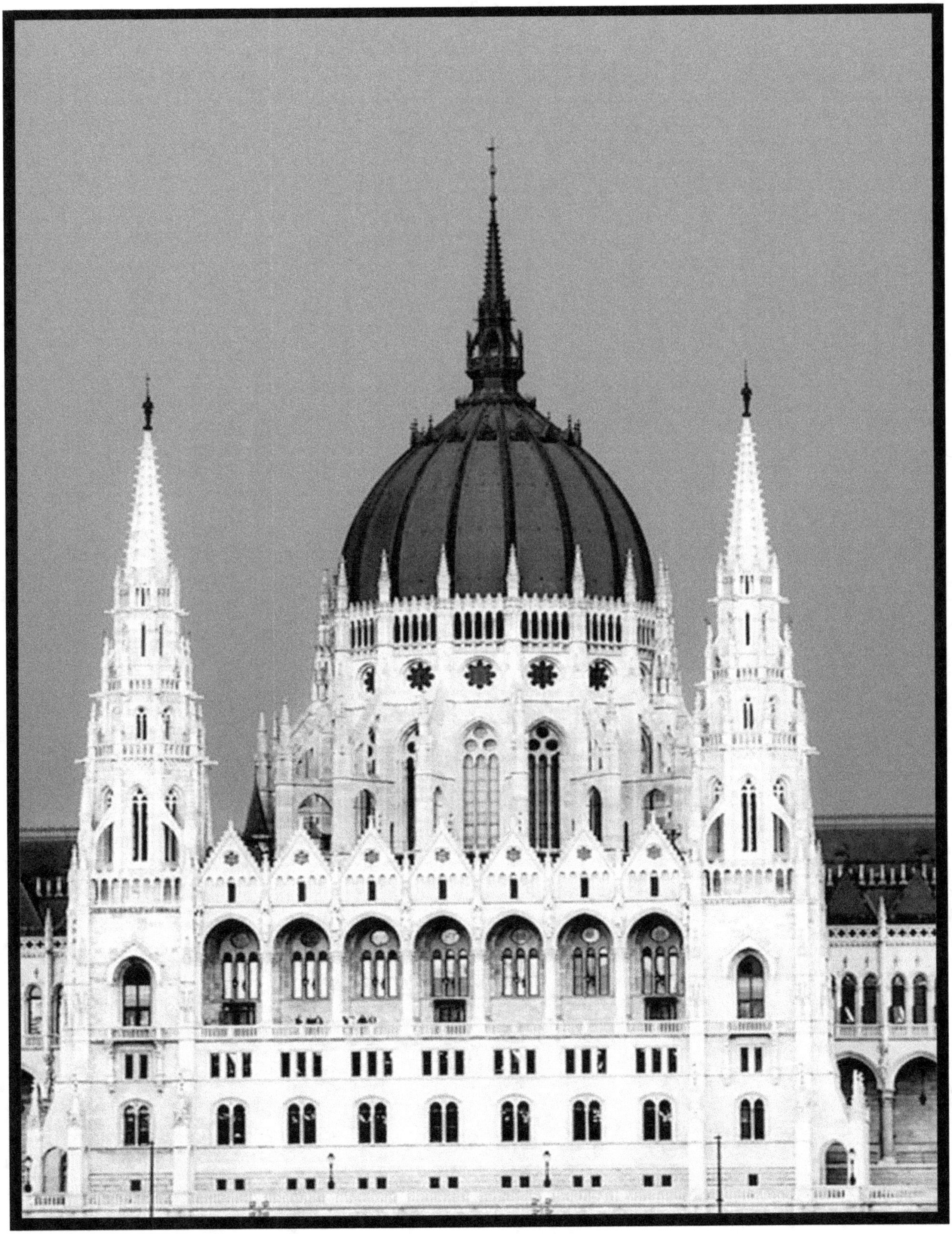

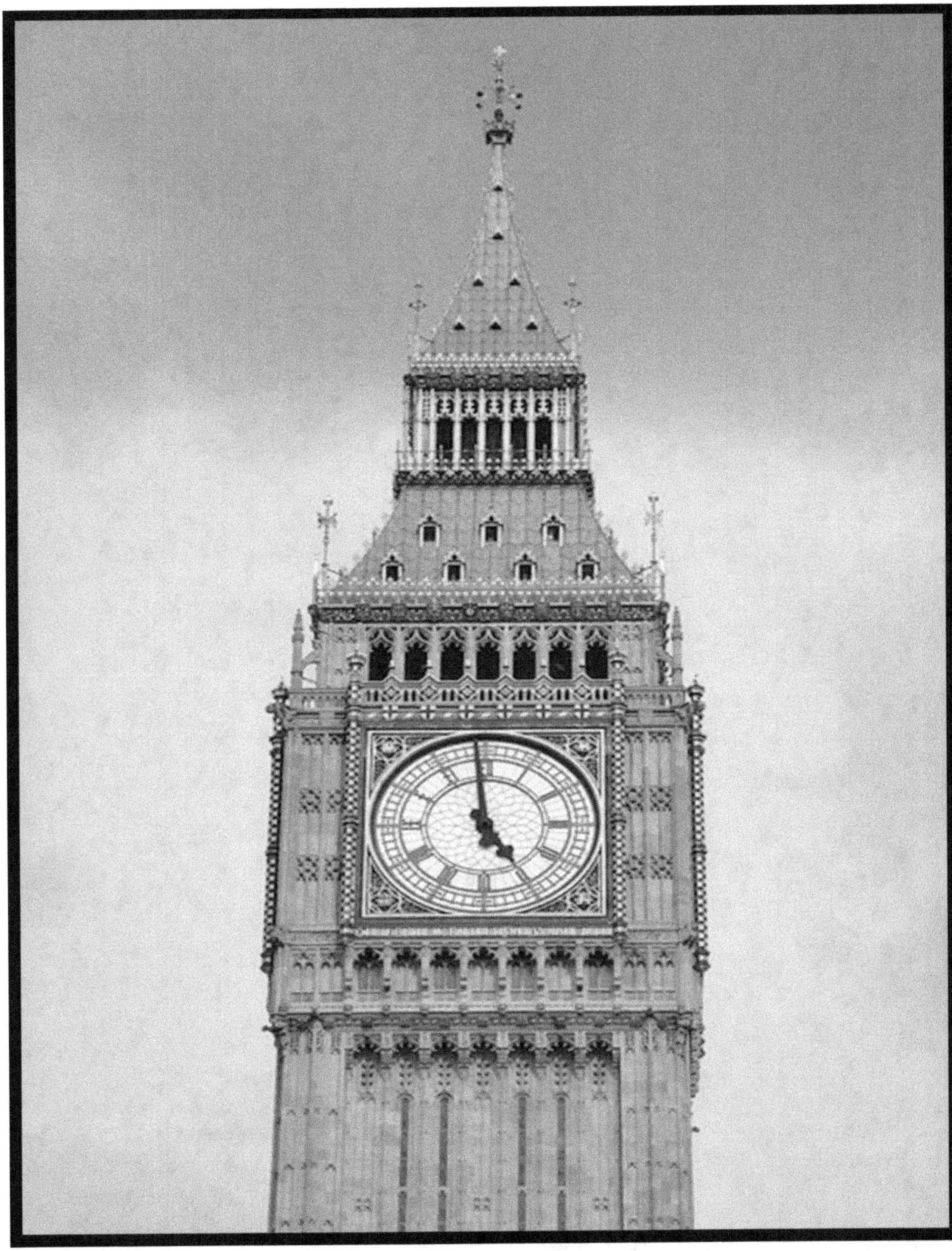

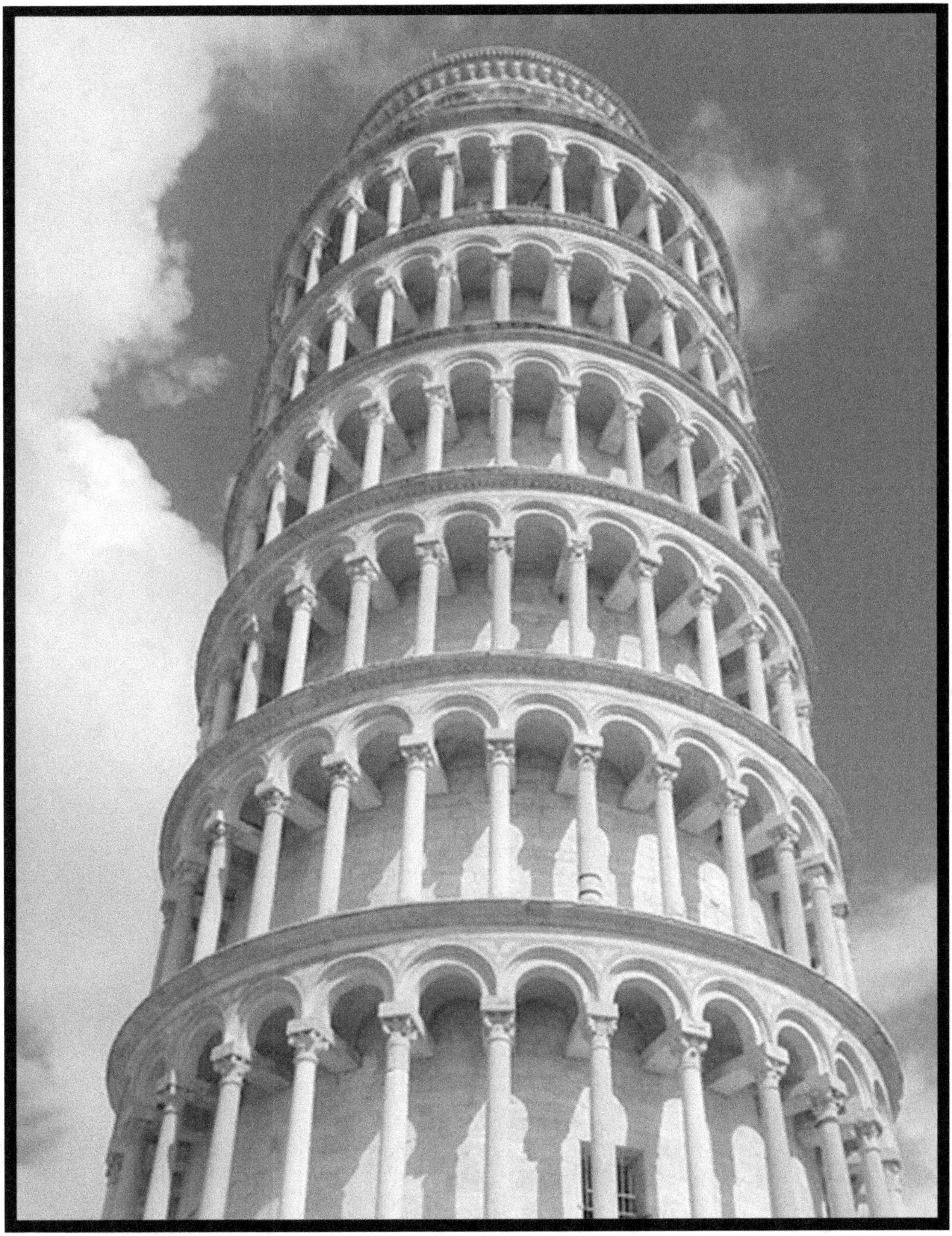

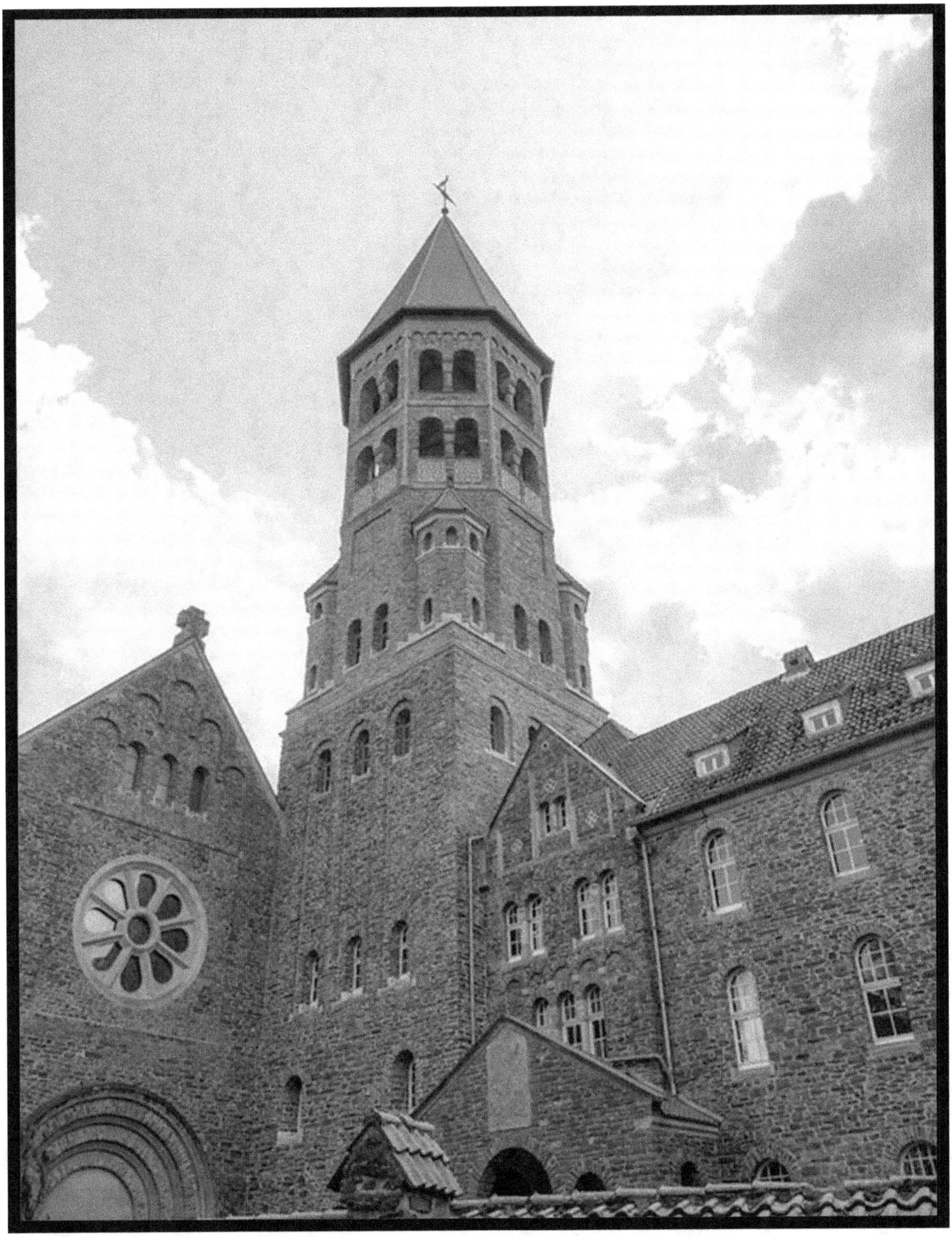

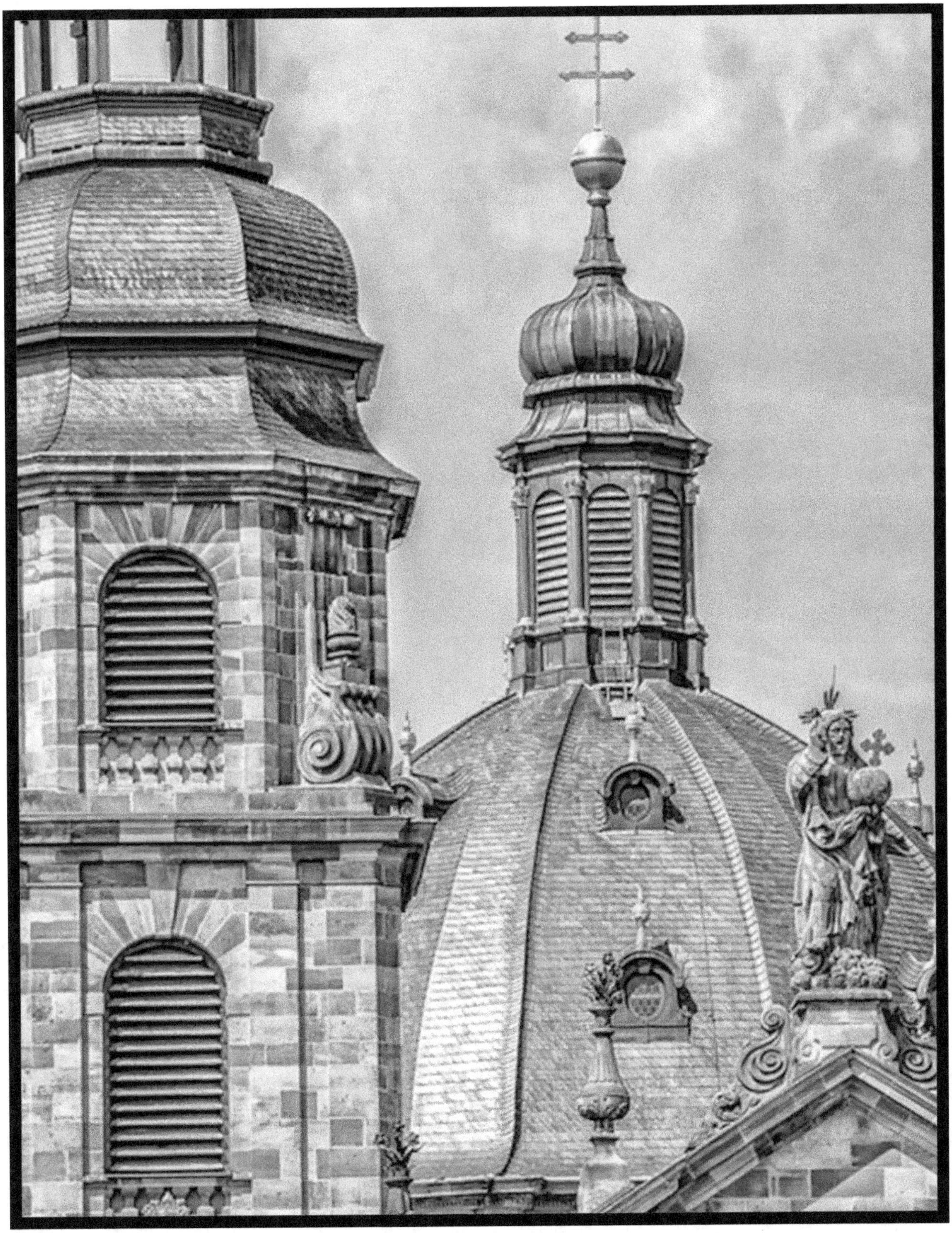

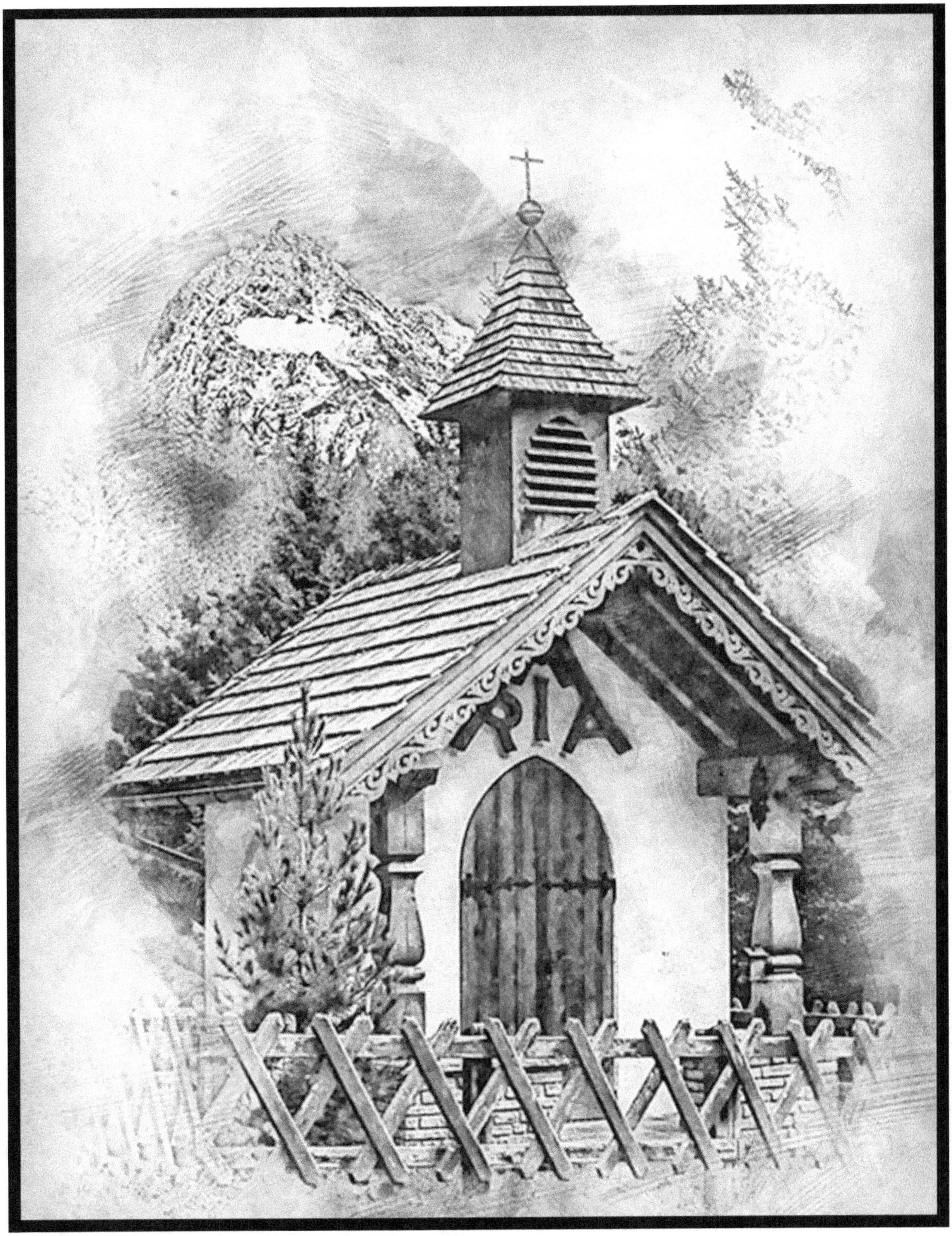
RIA

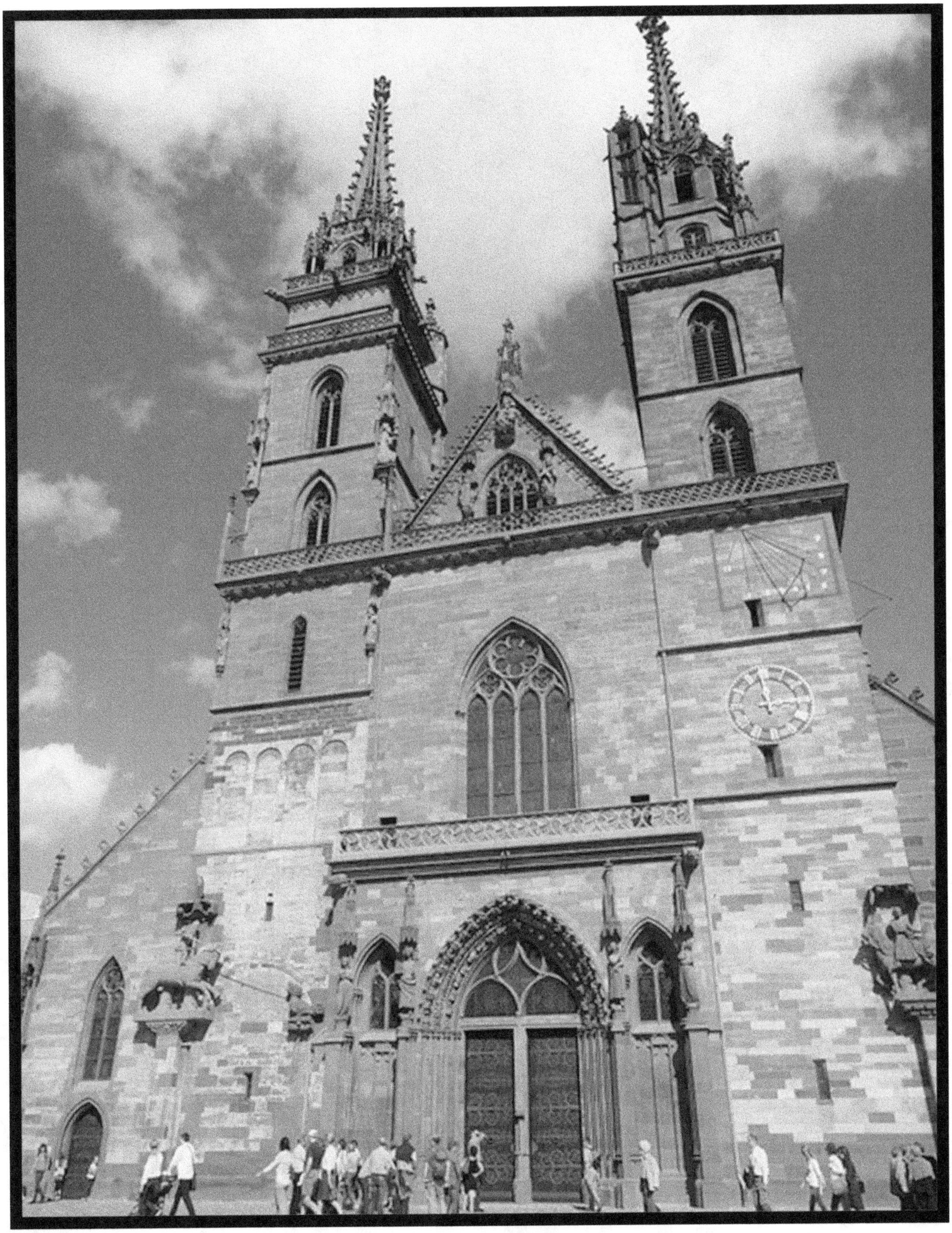

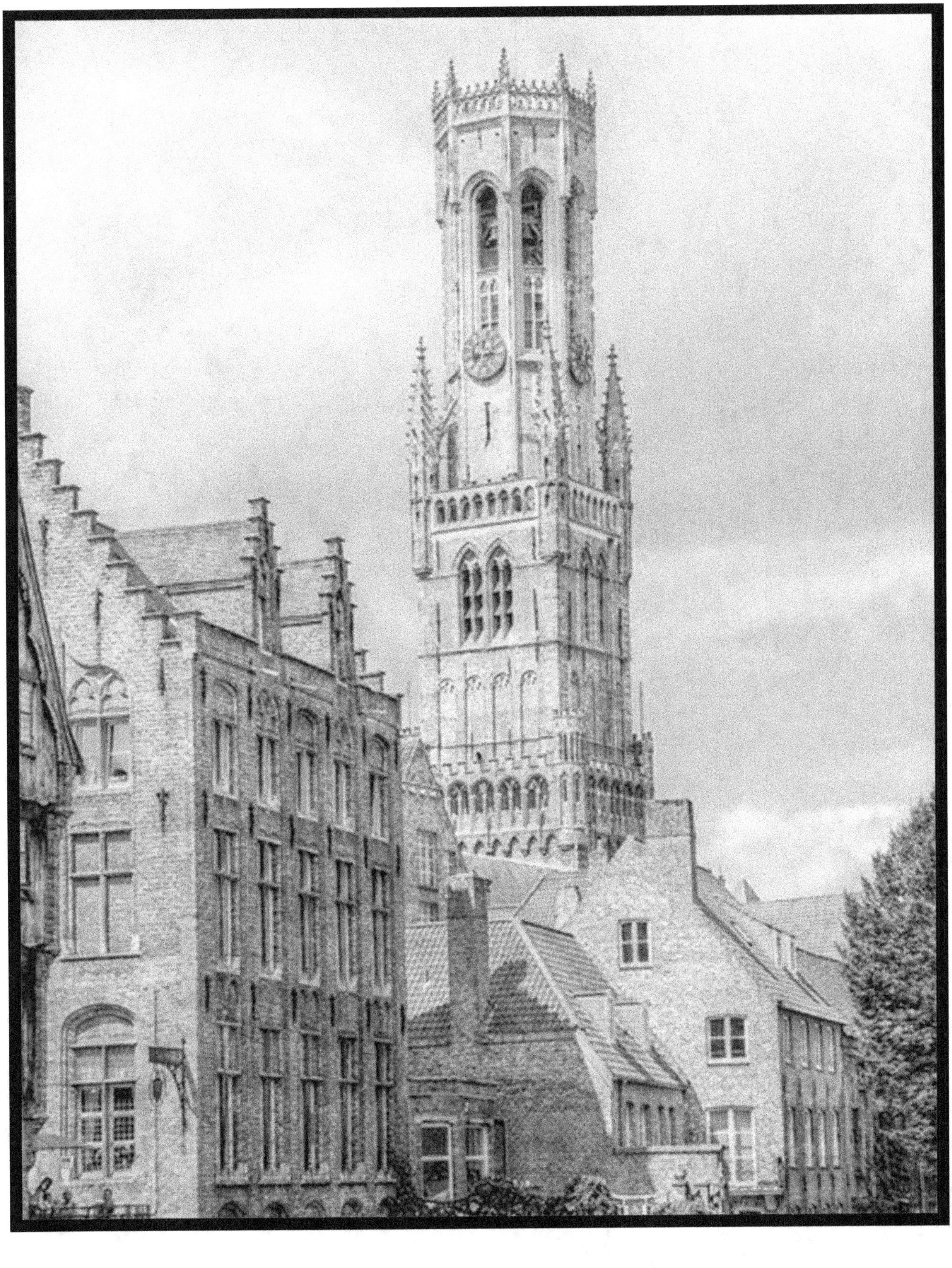

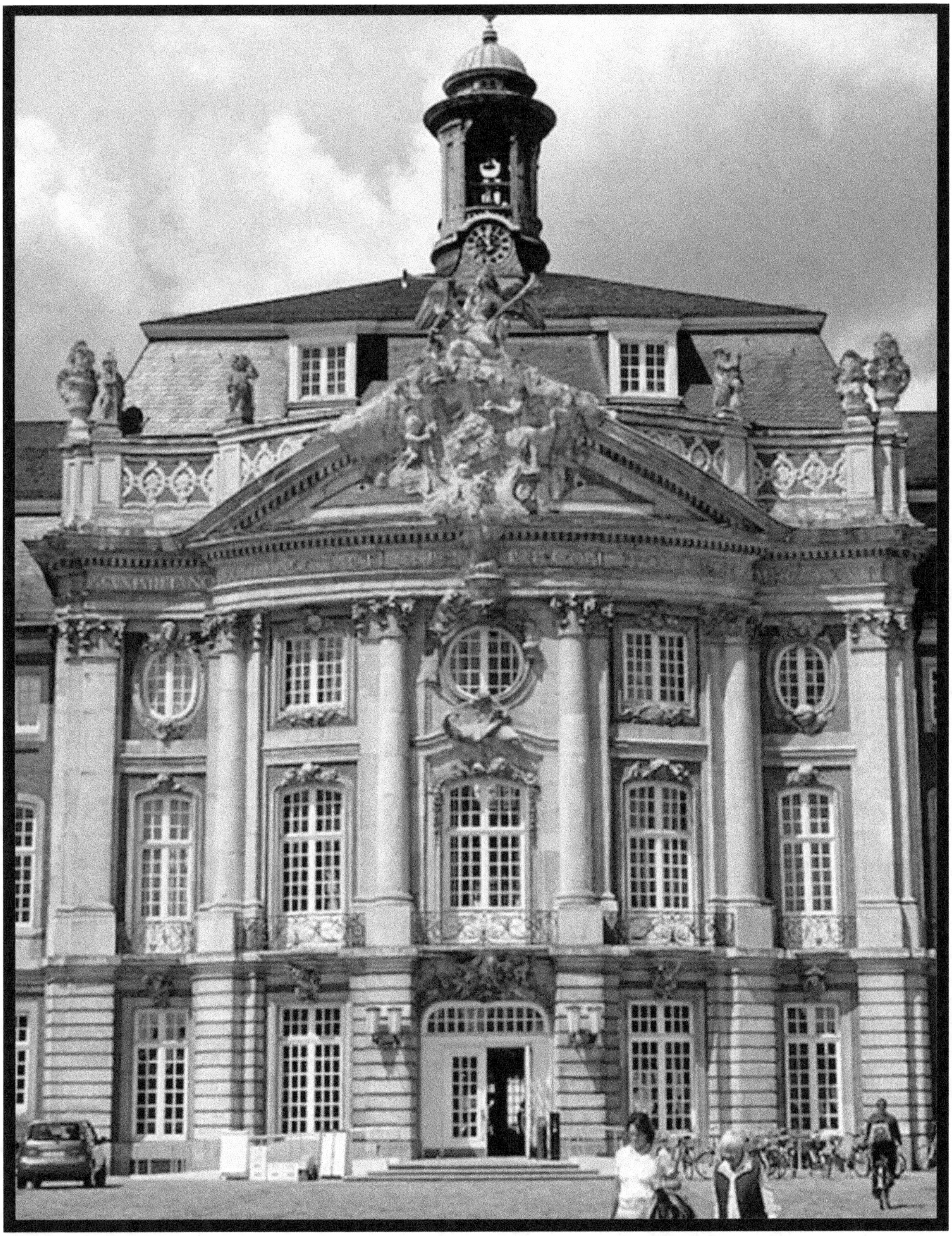

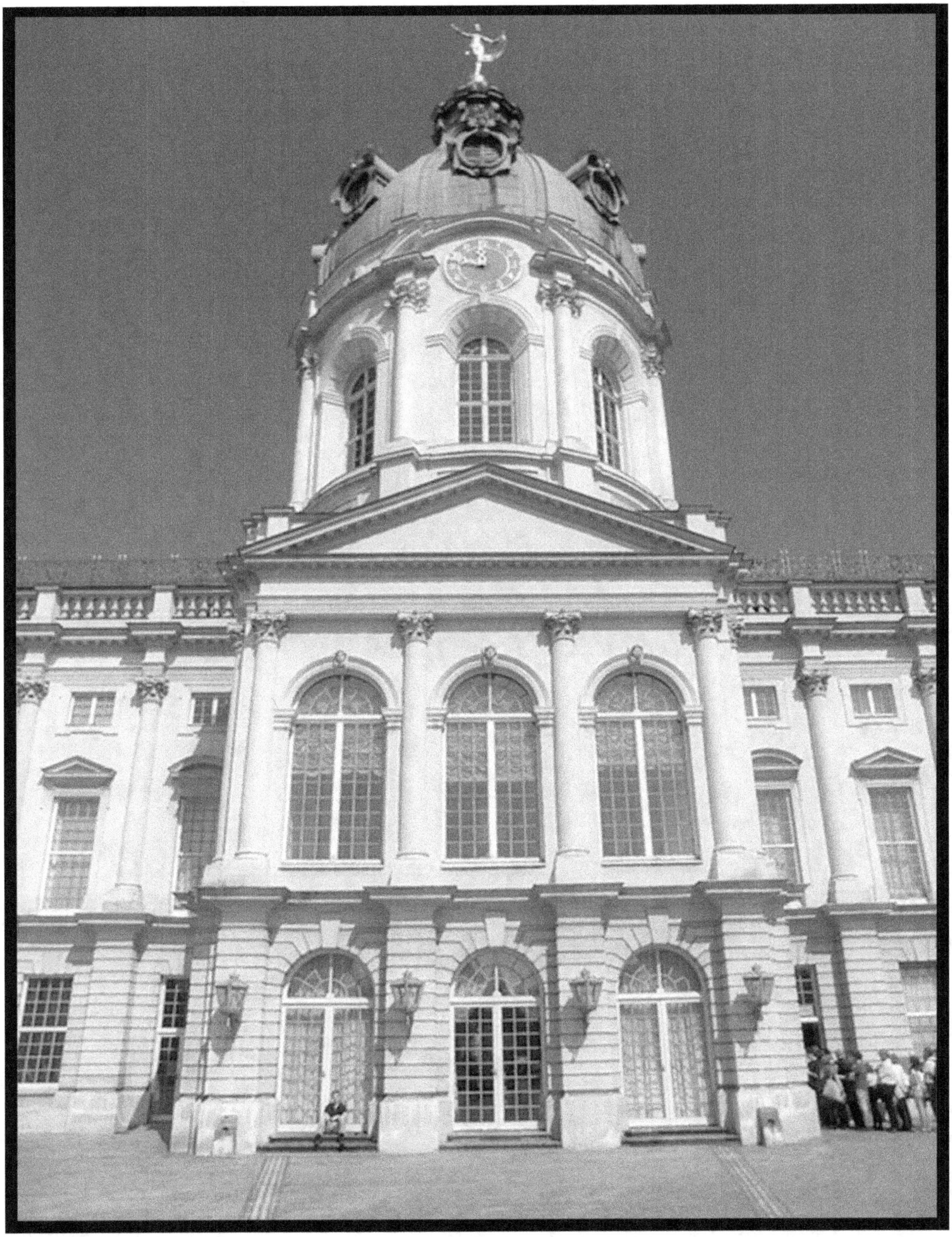

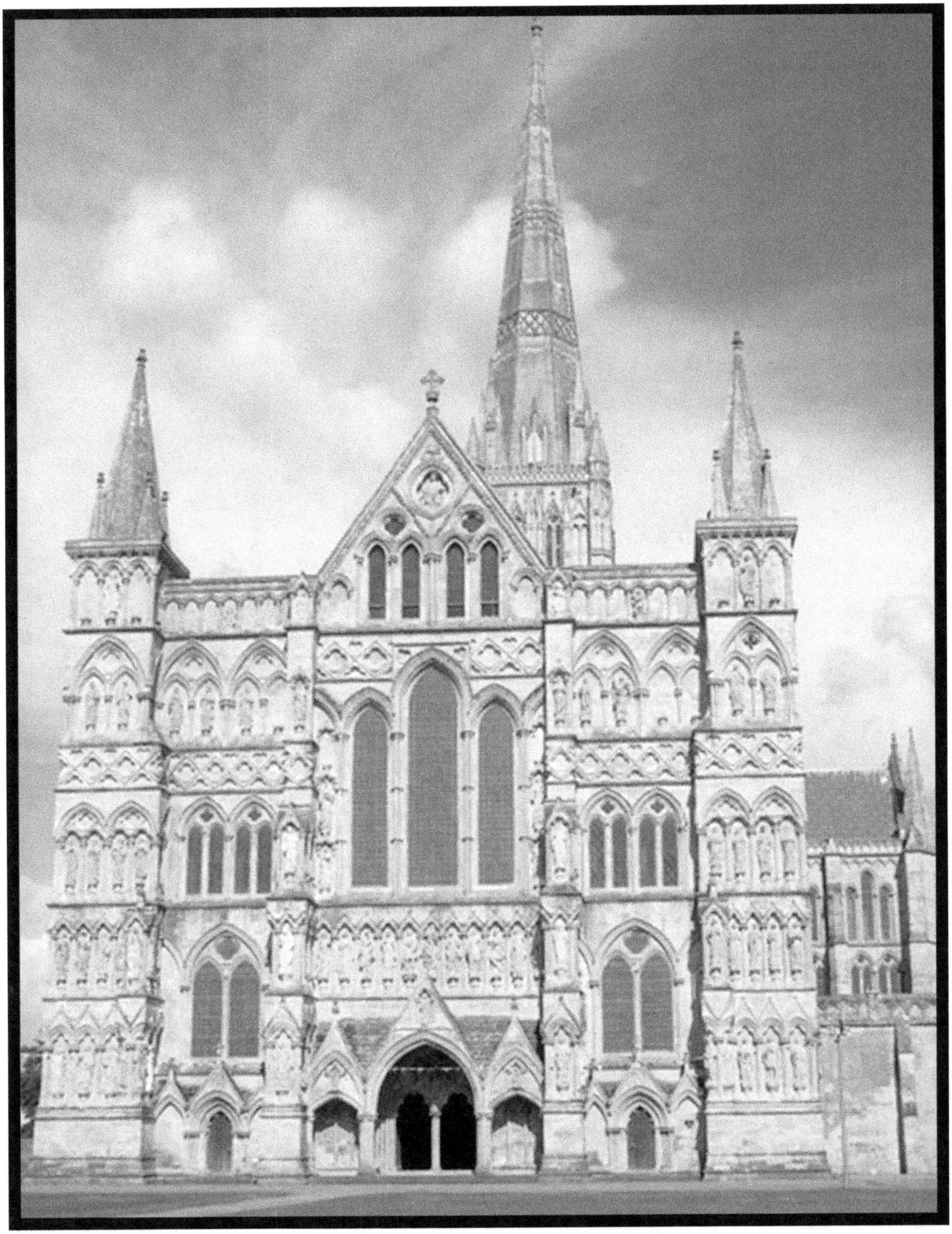

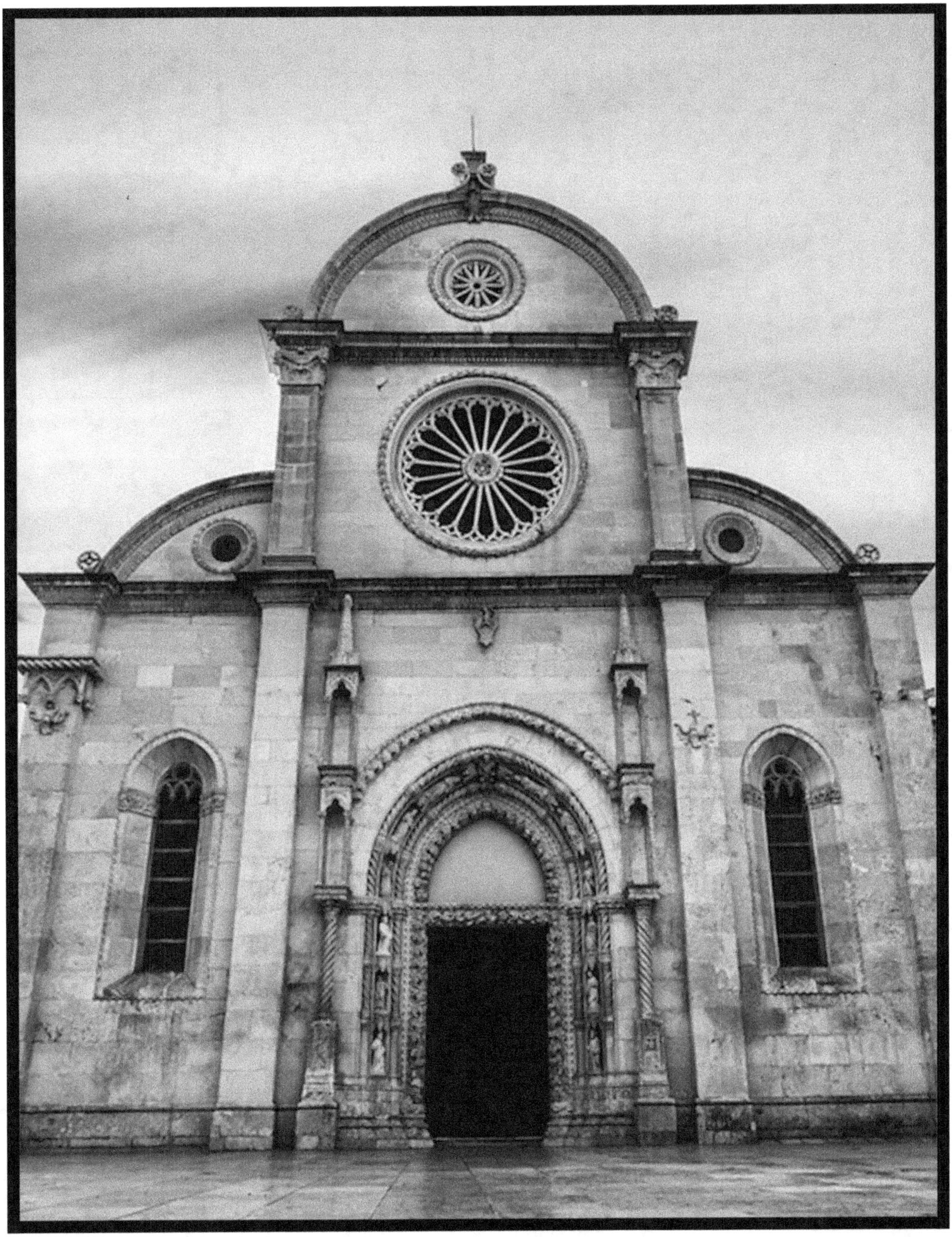

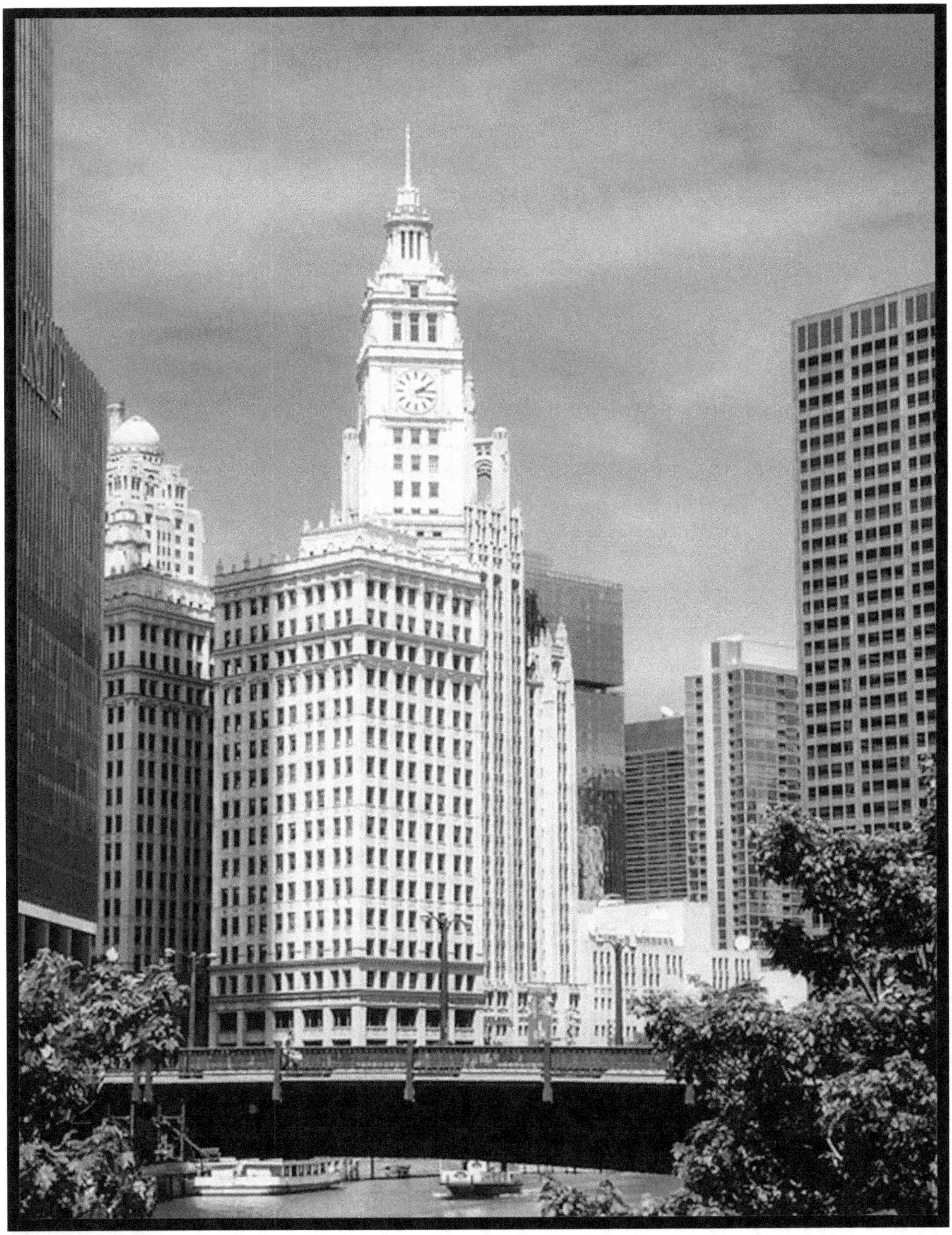

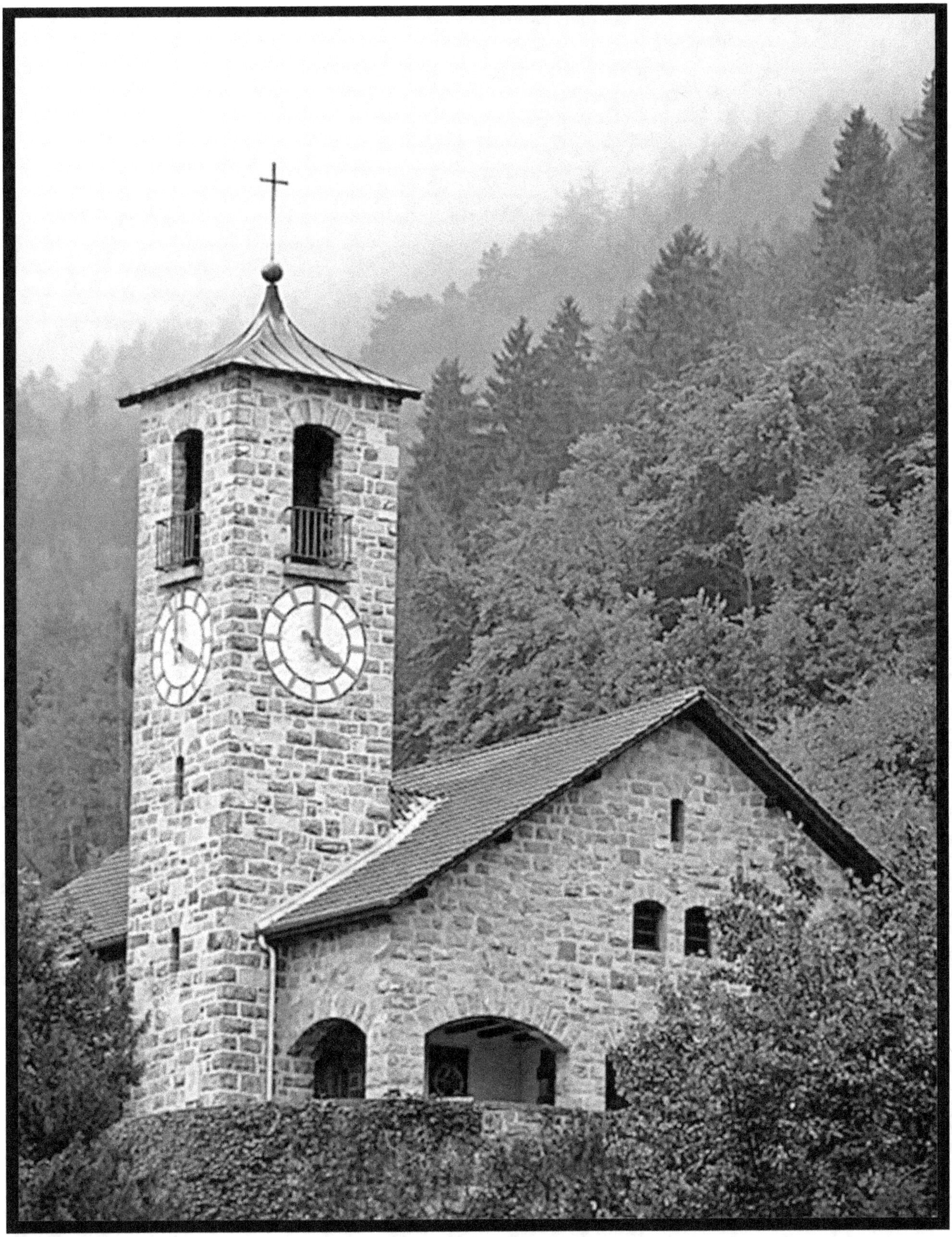

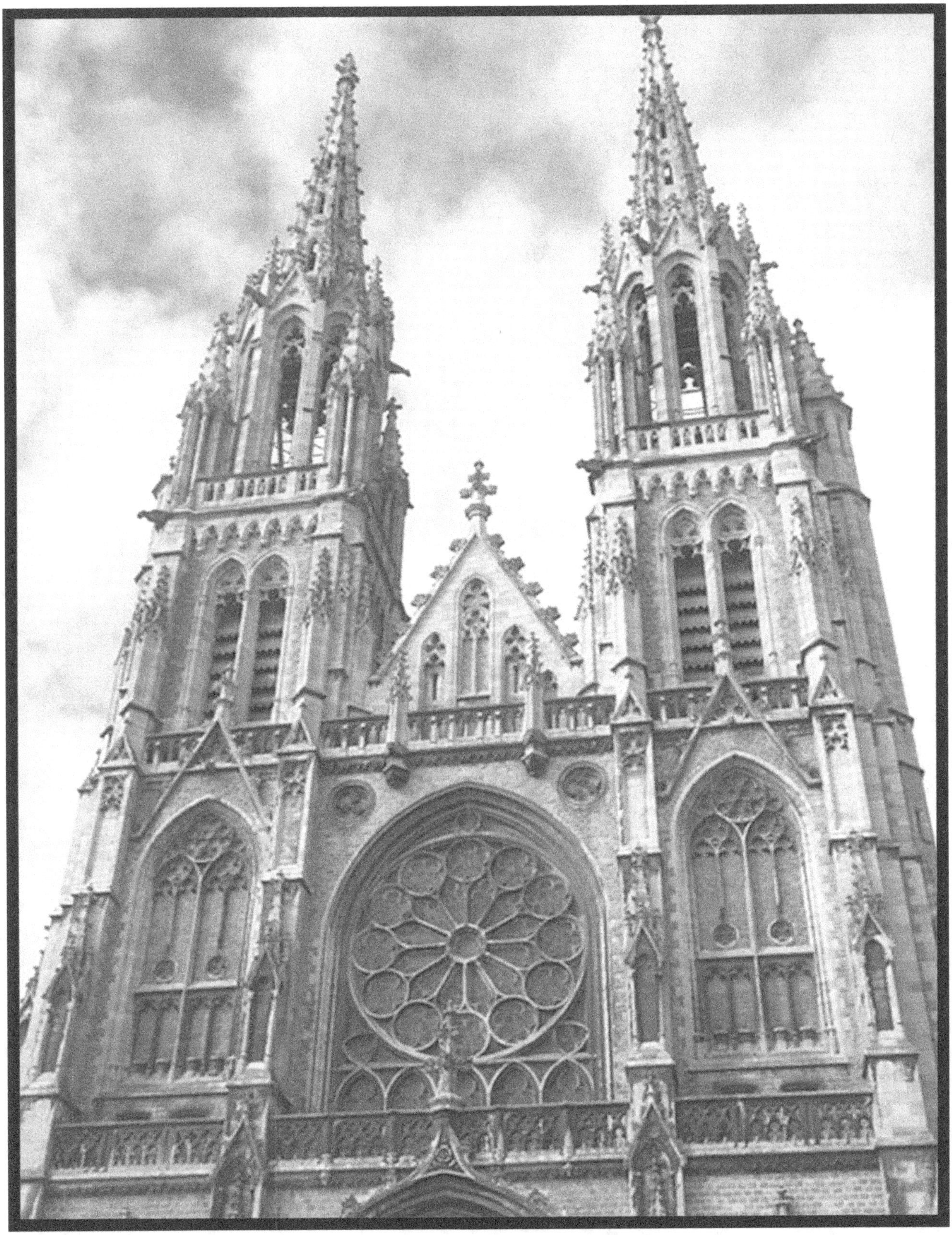

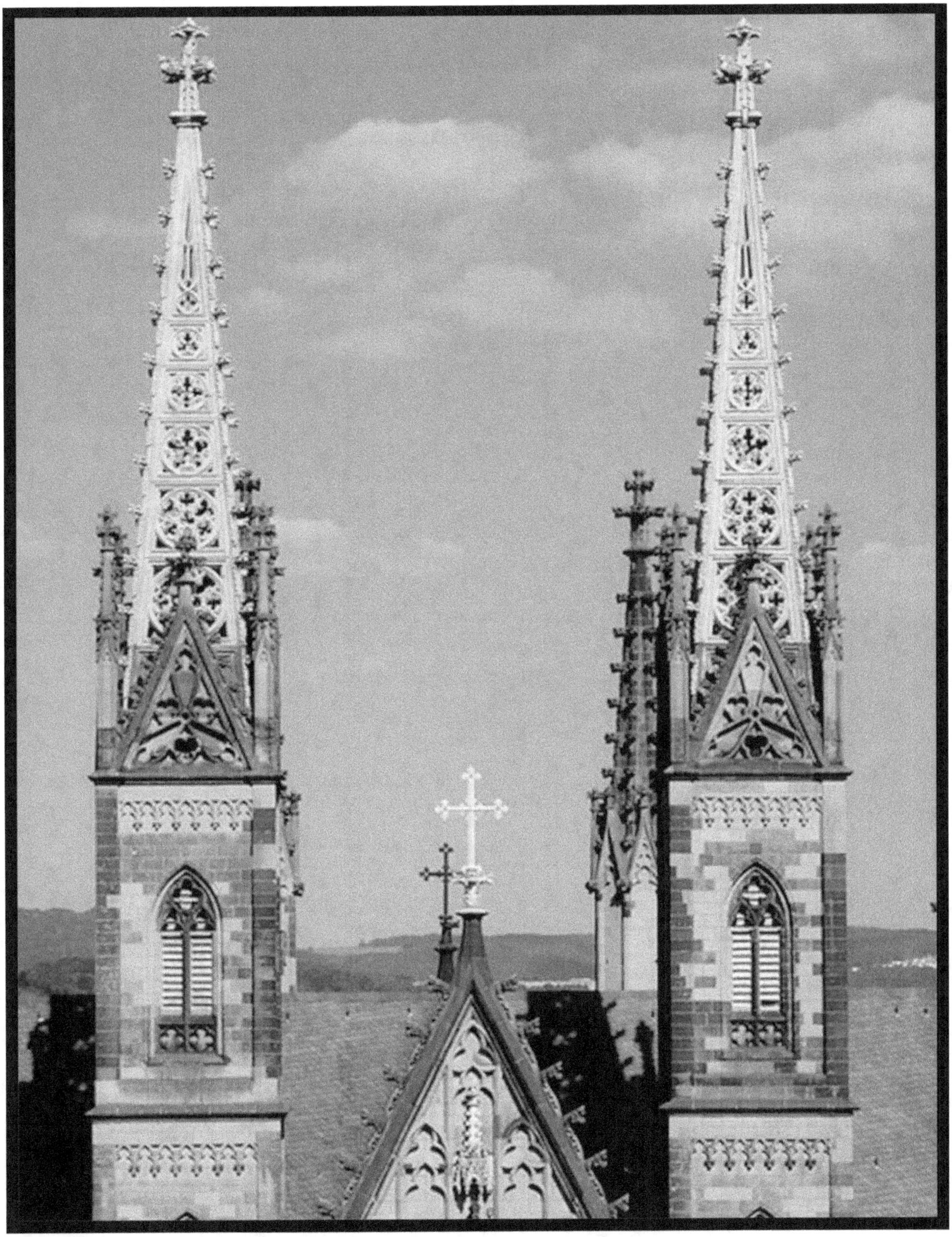

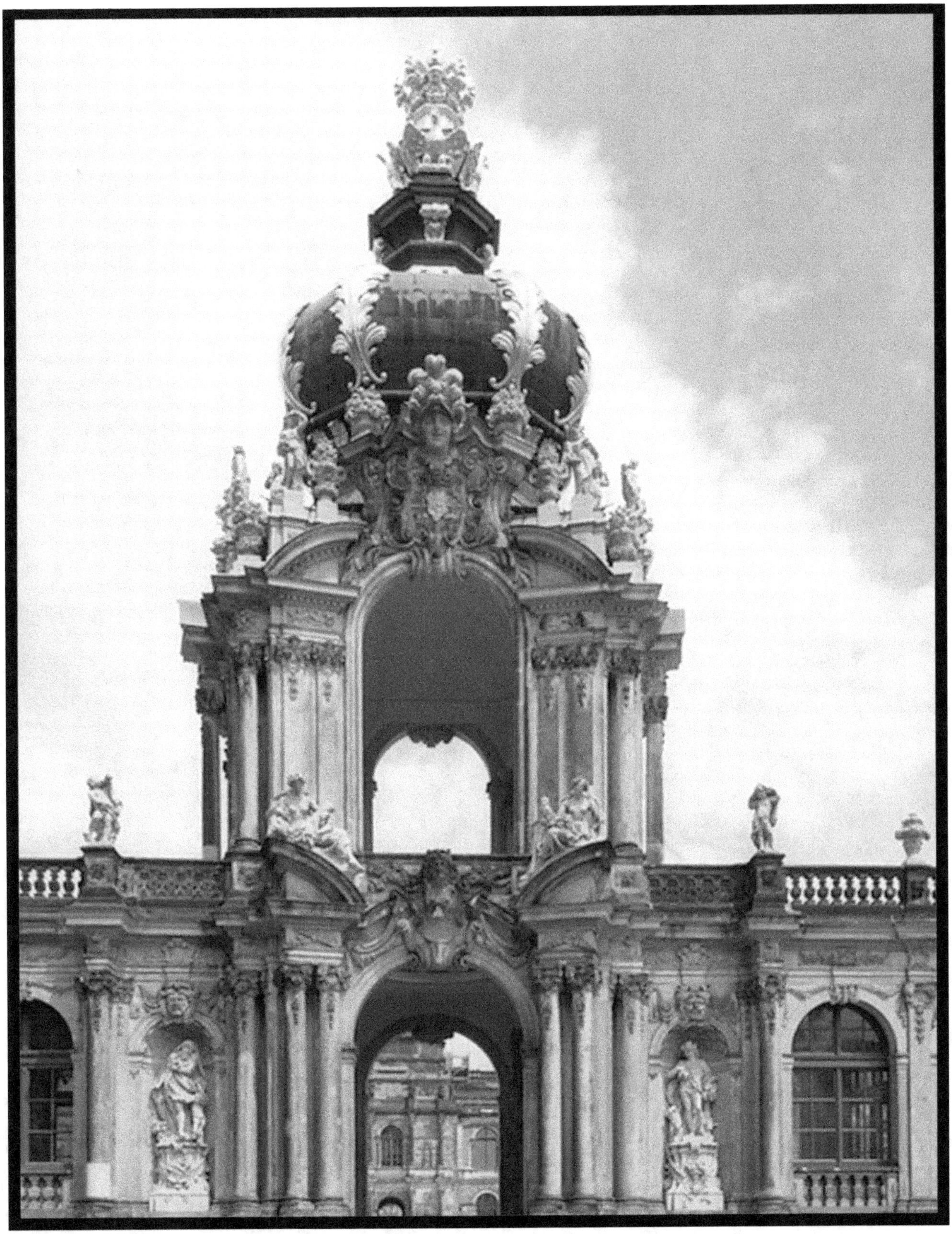

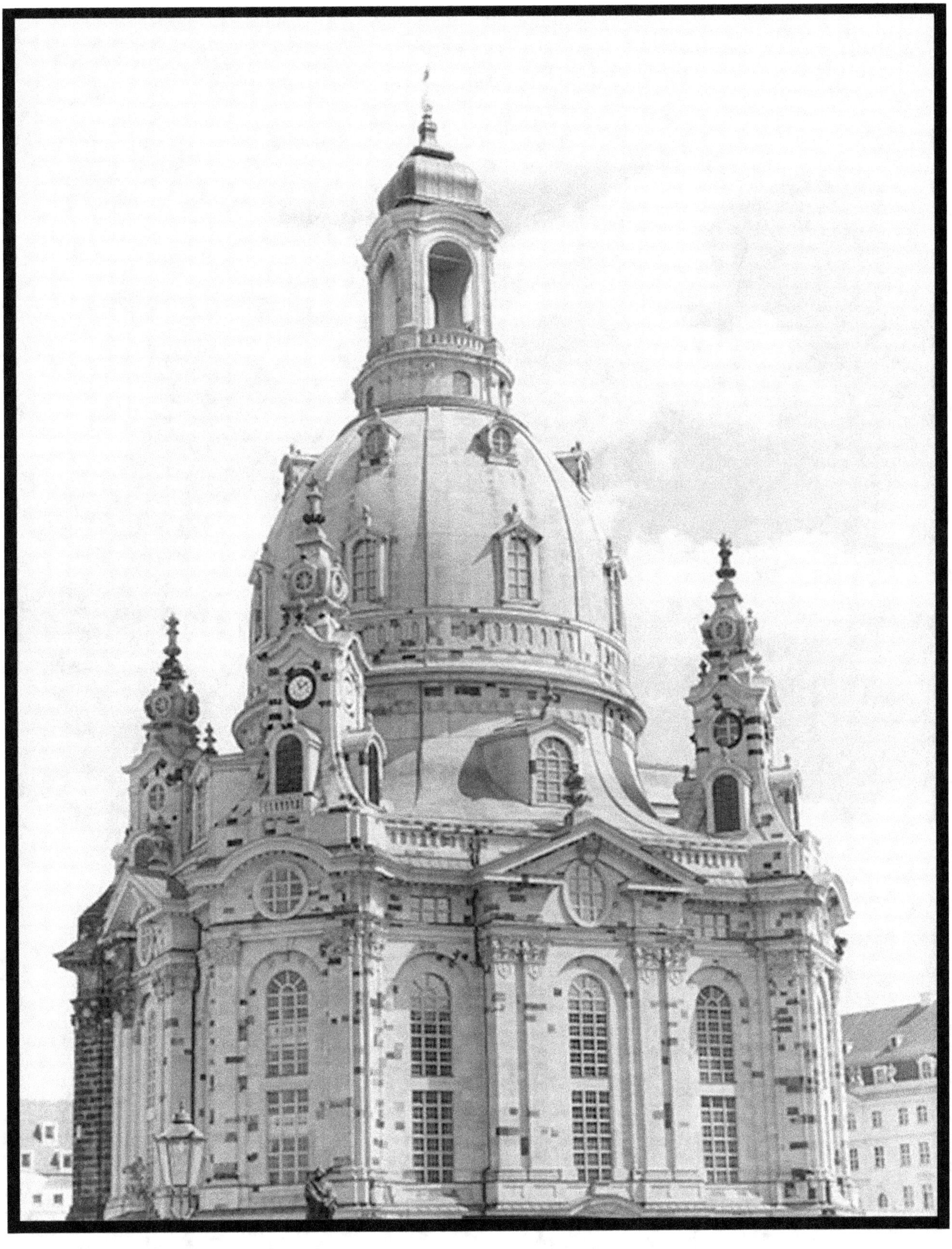

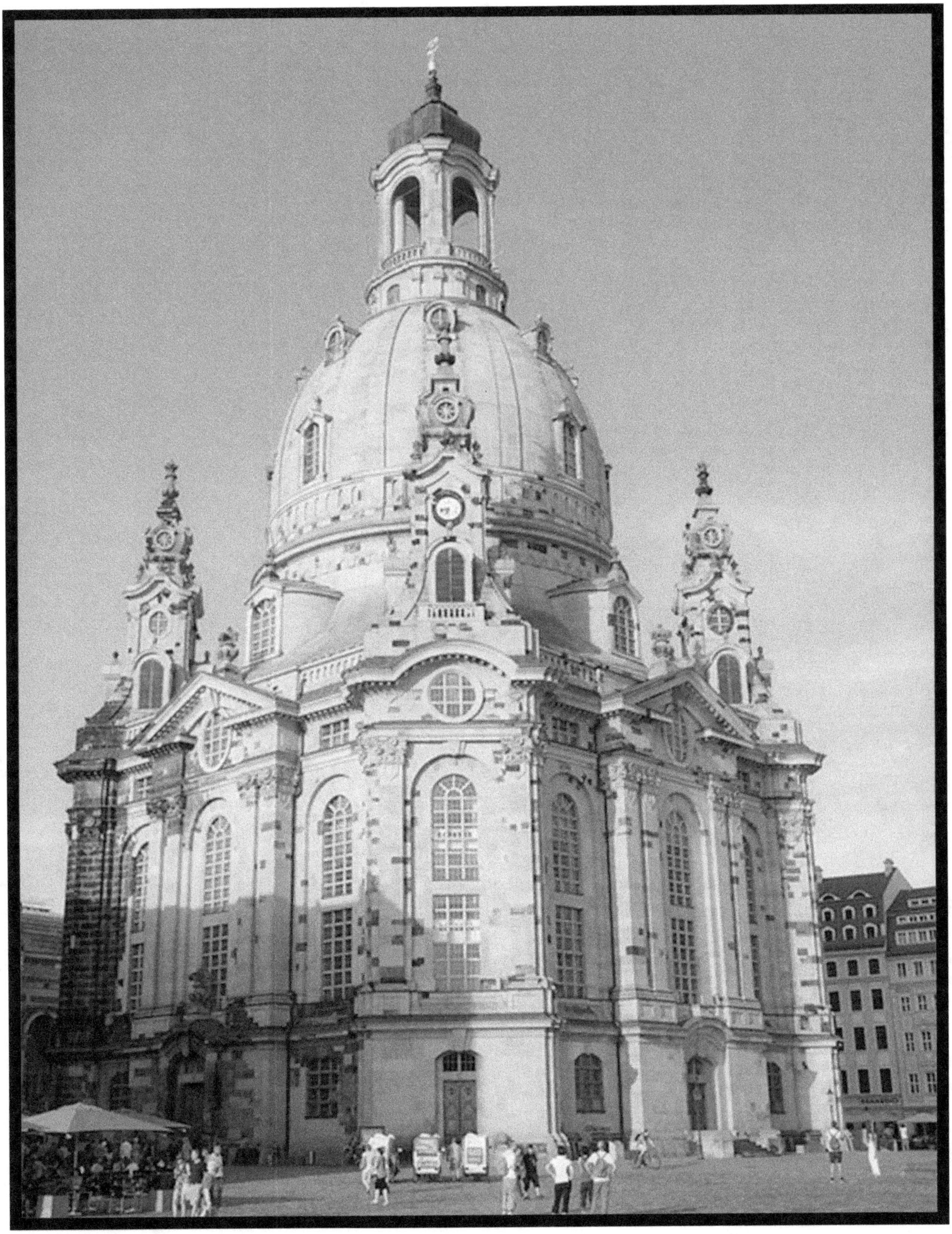

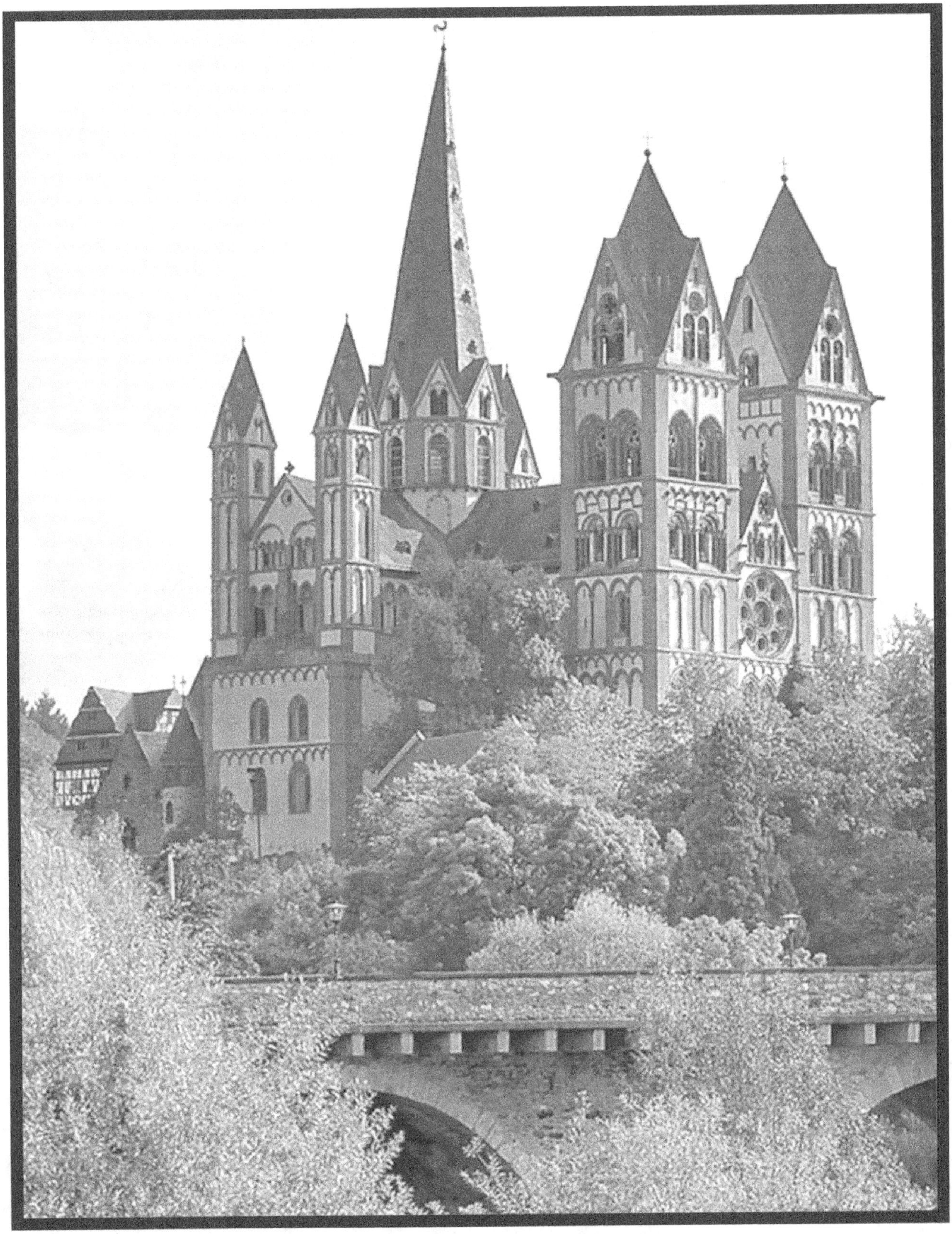

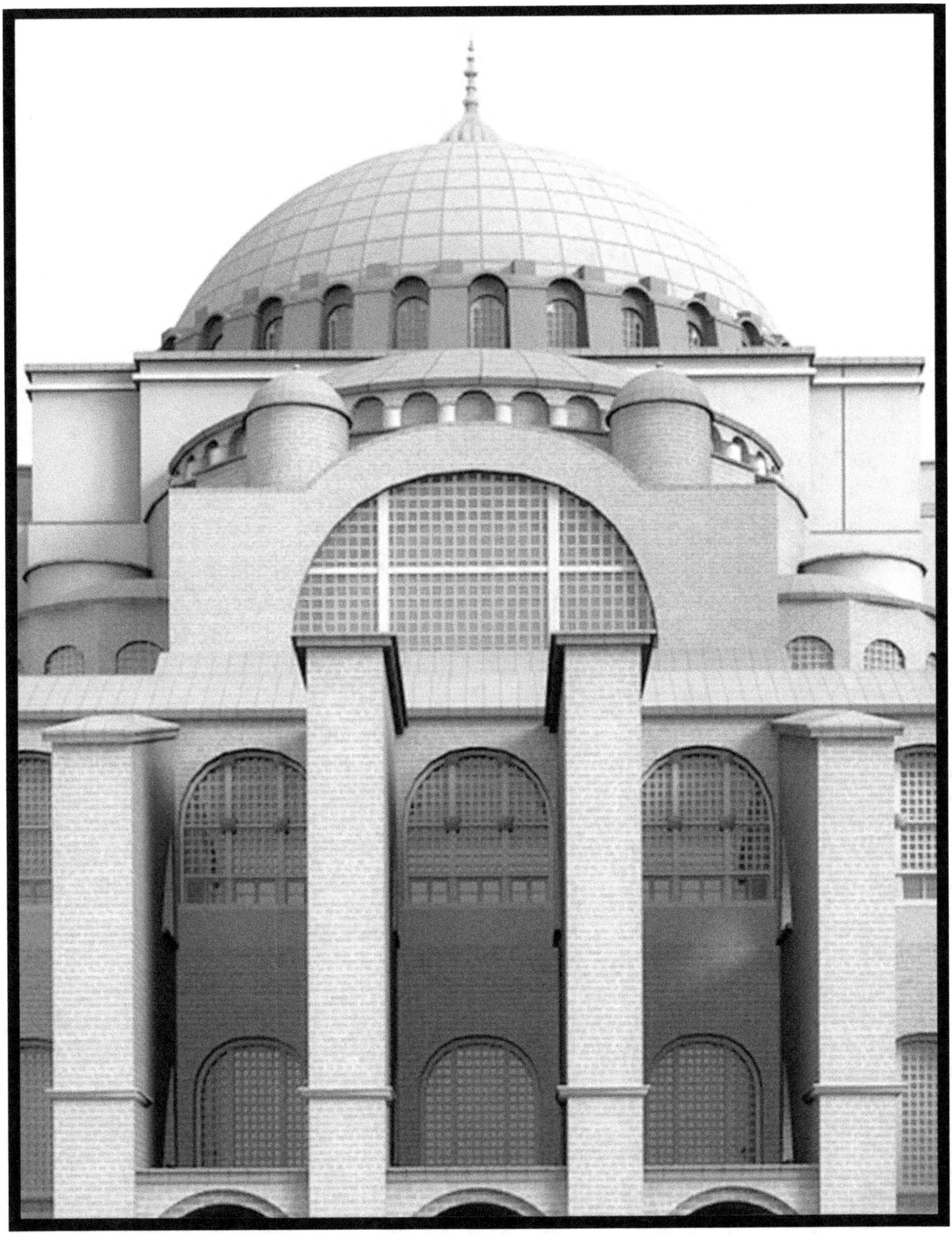

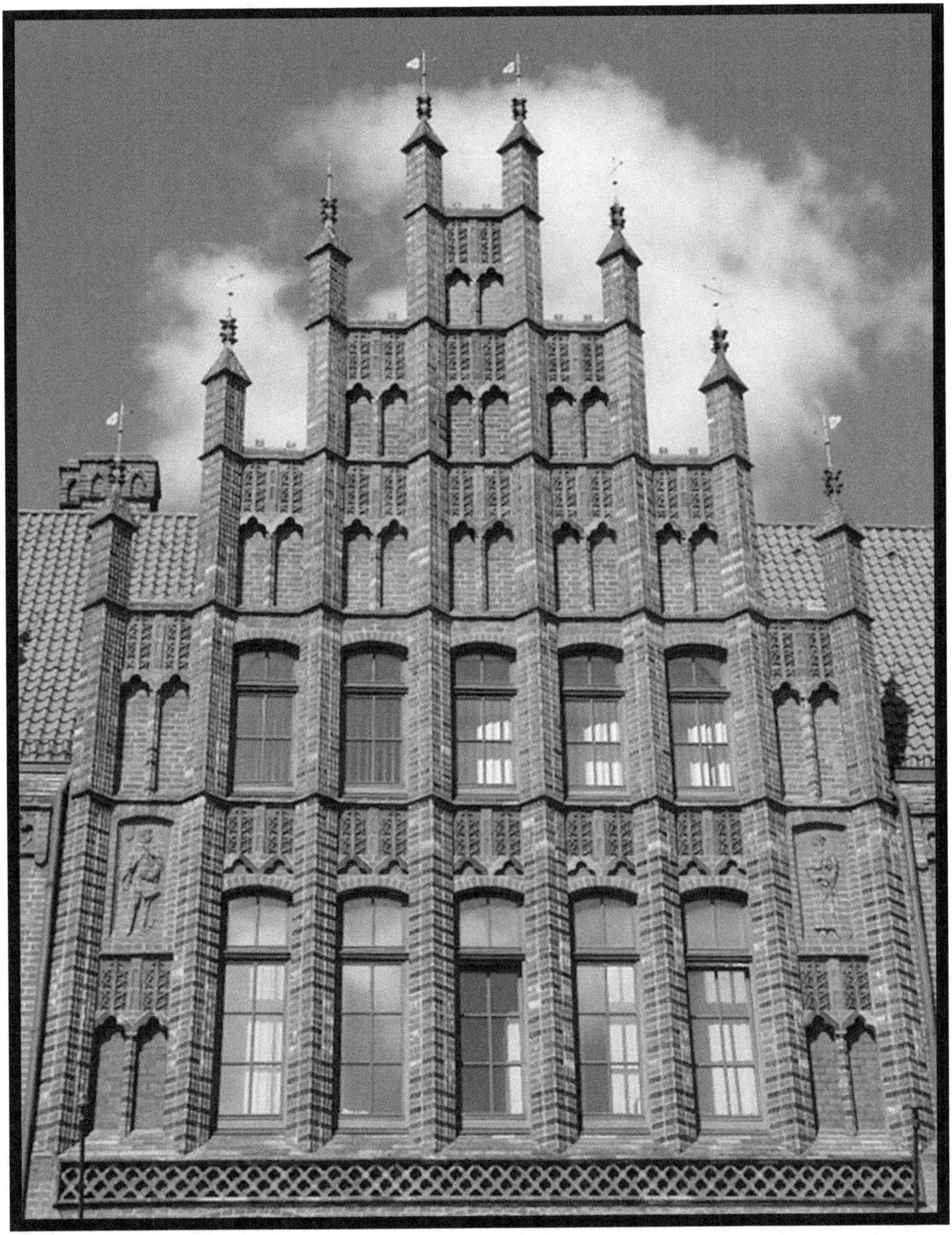

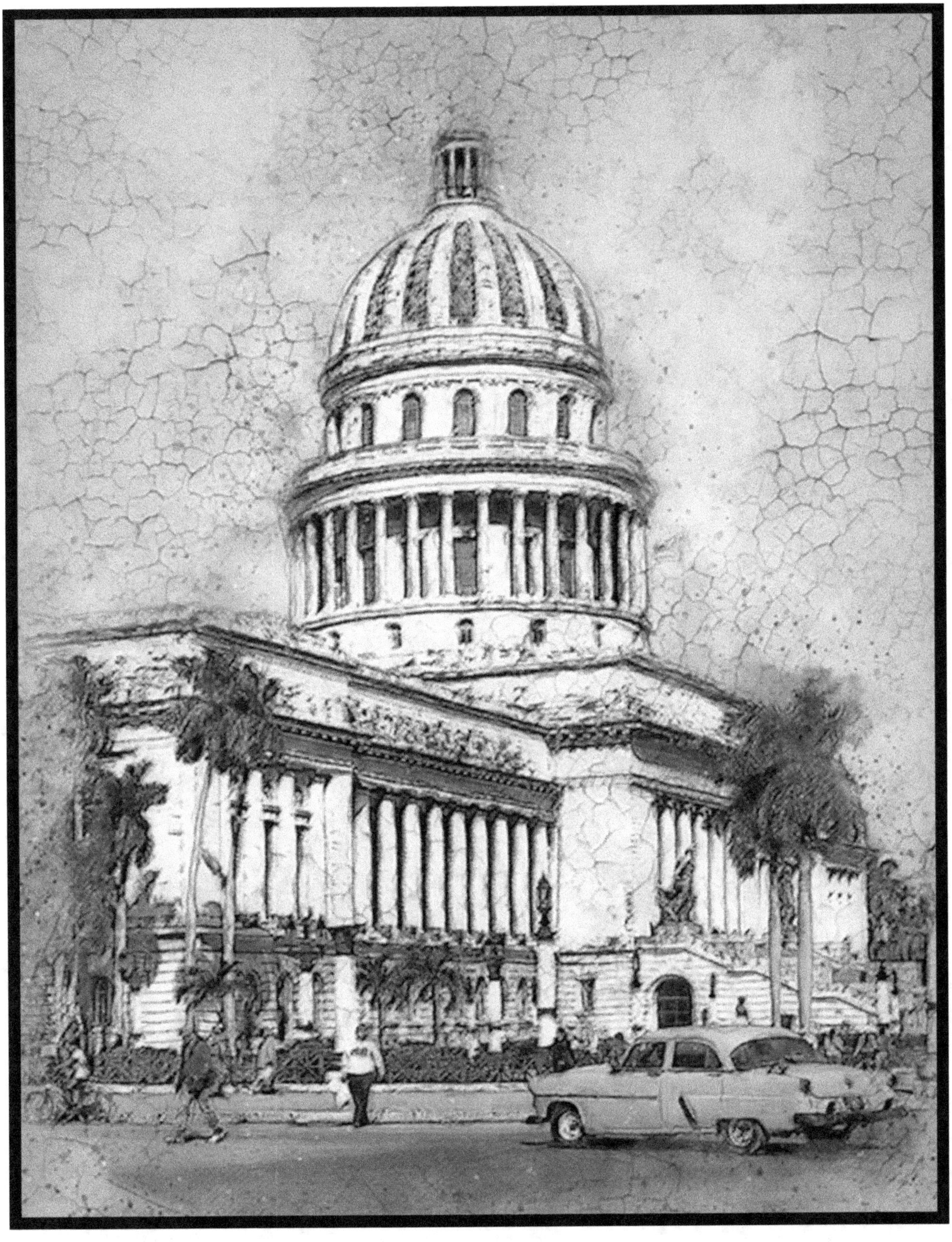

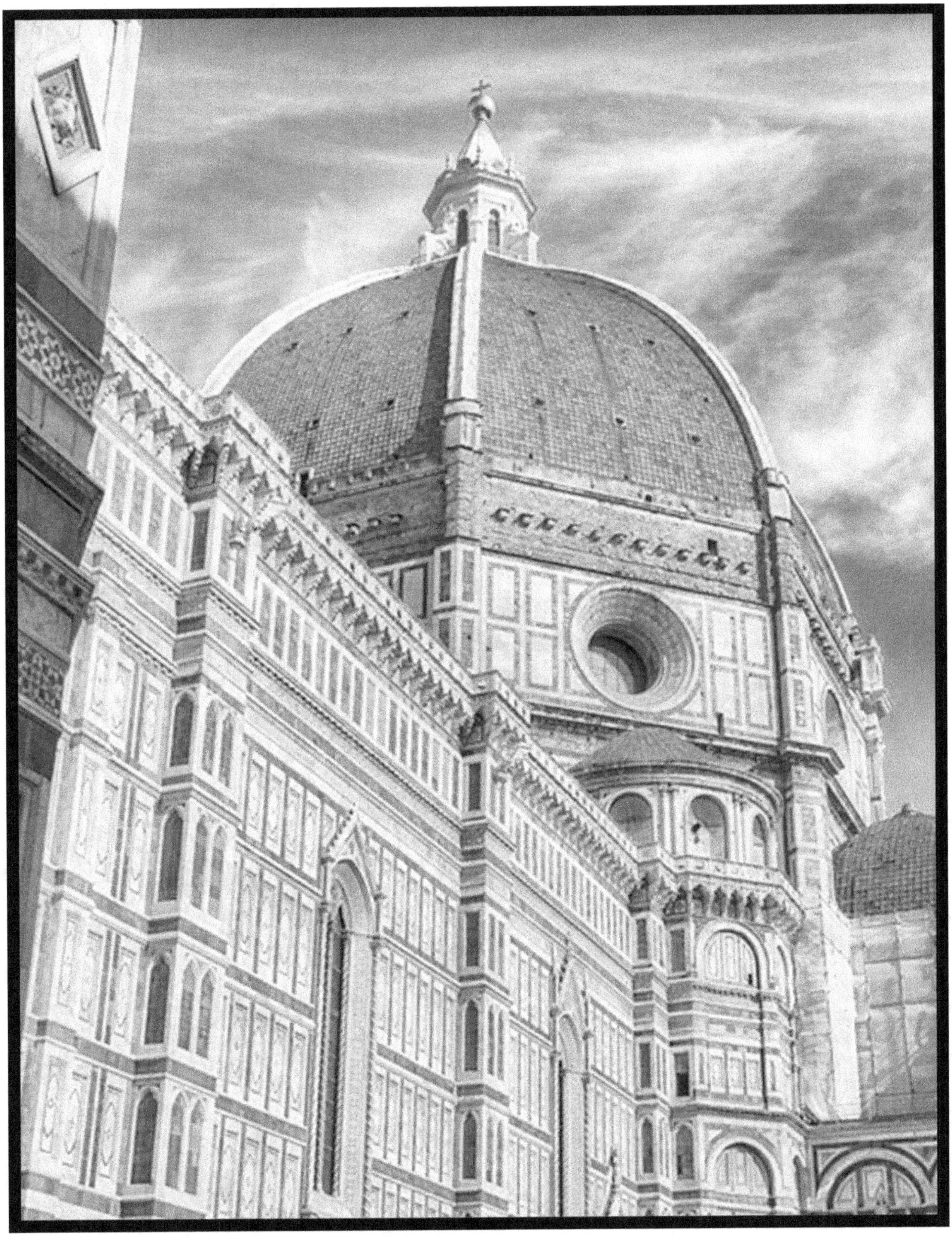

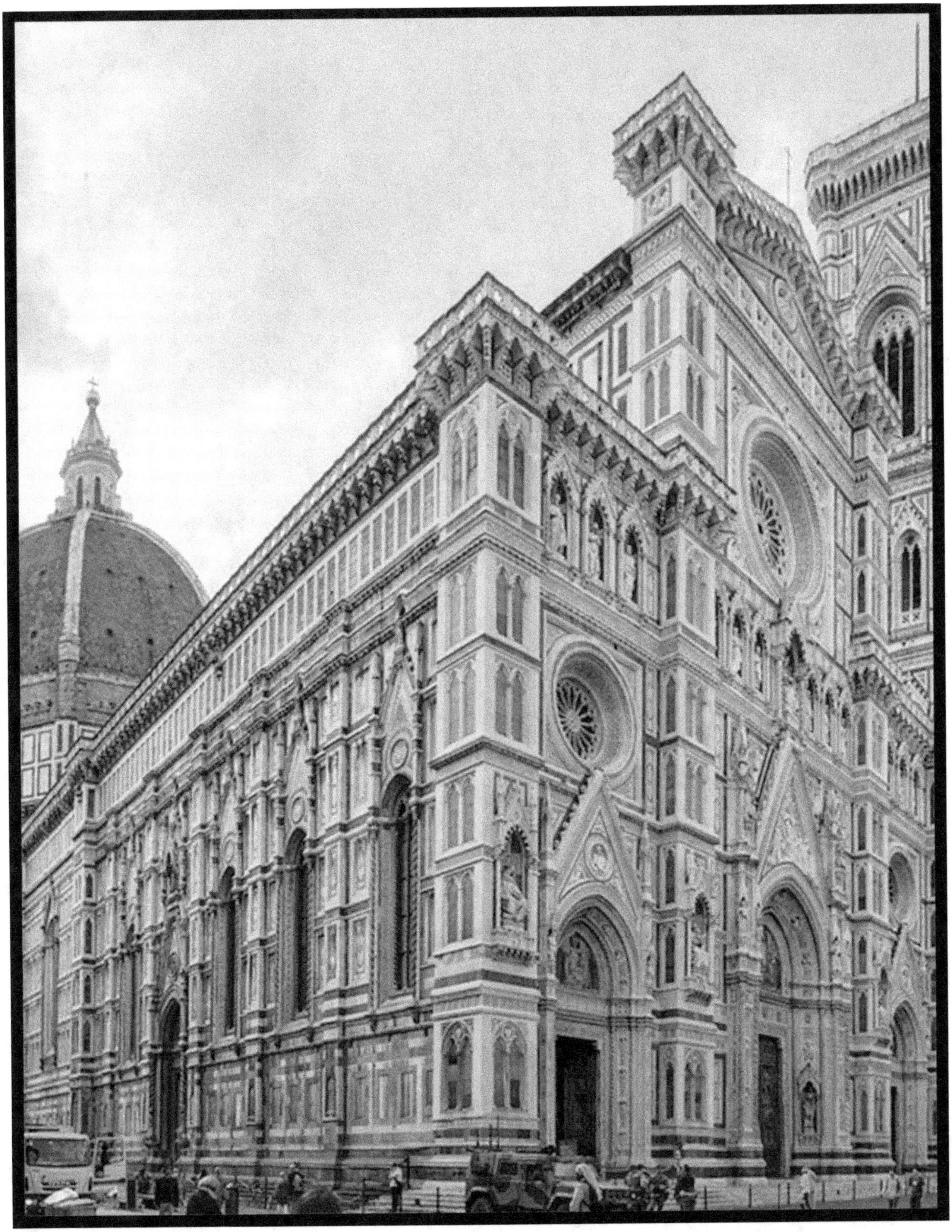

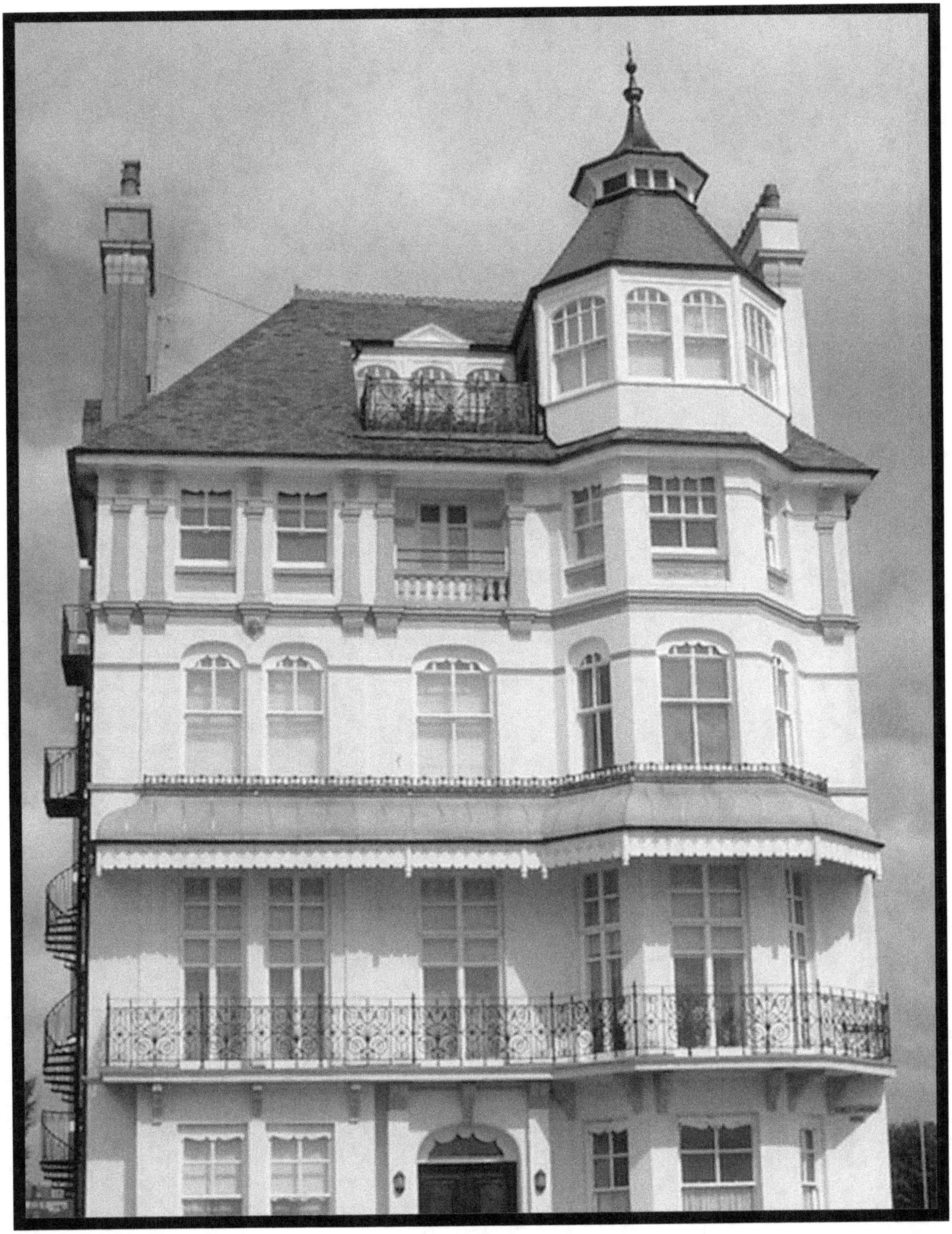

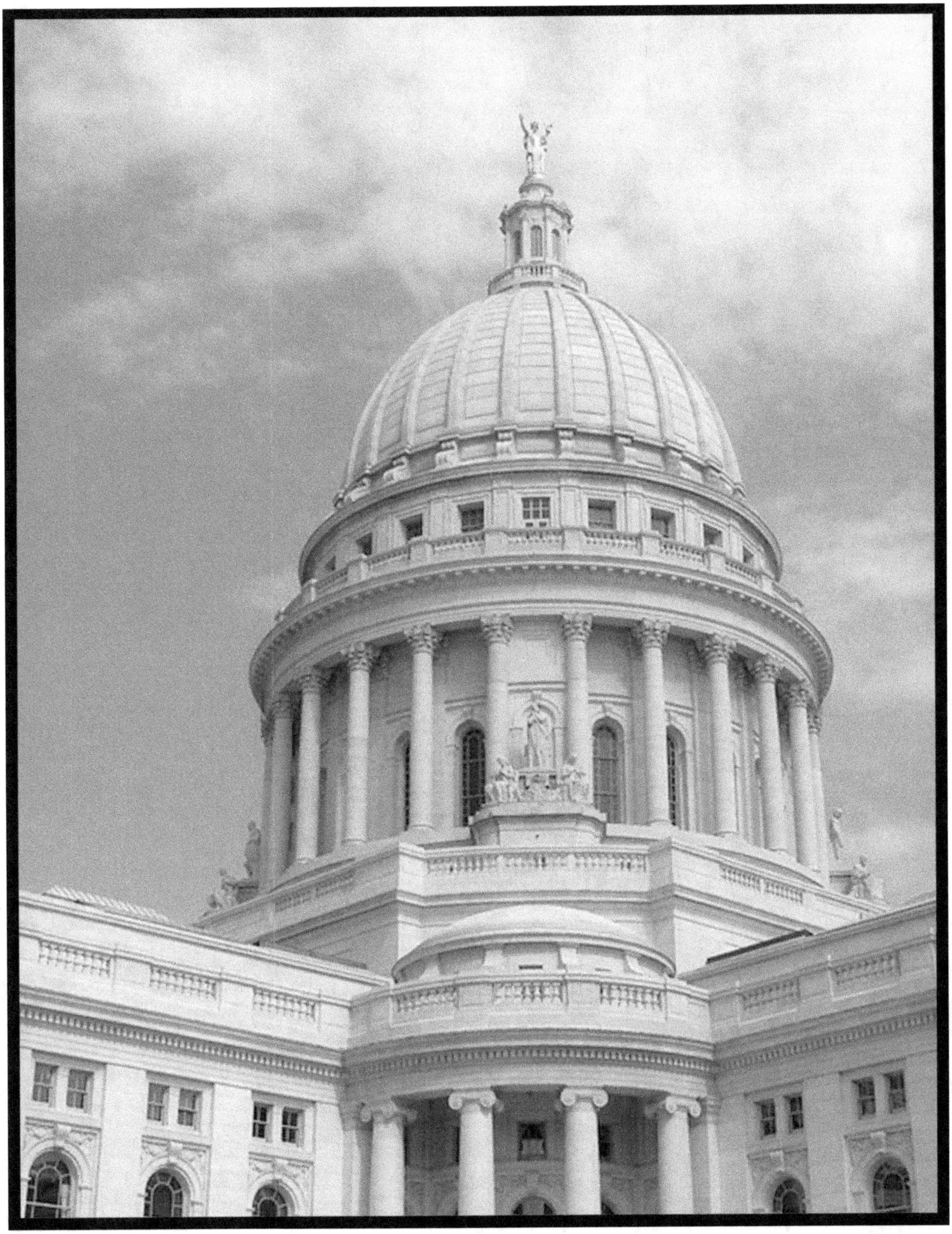

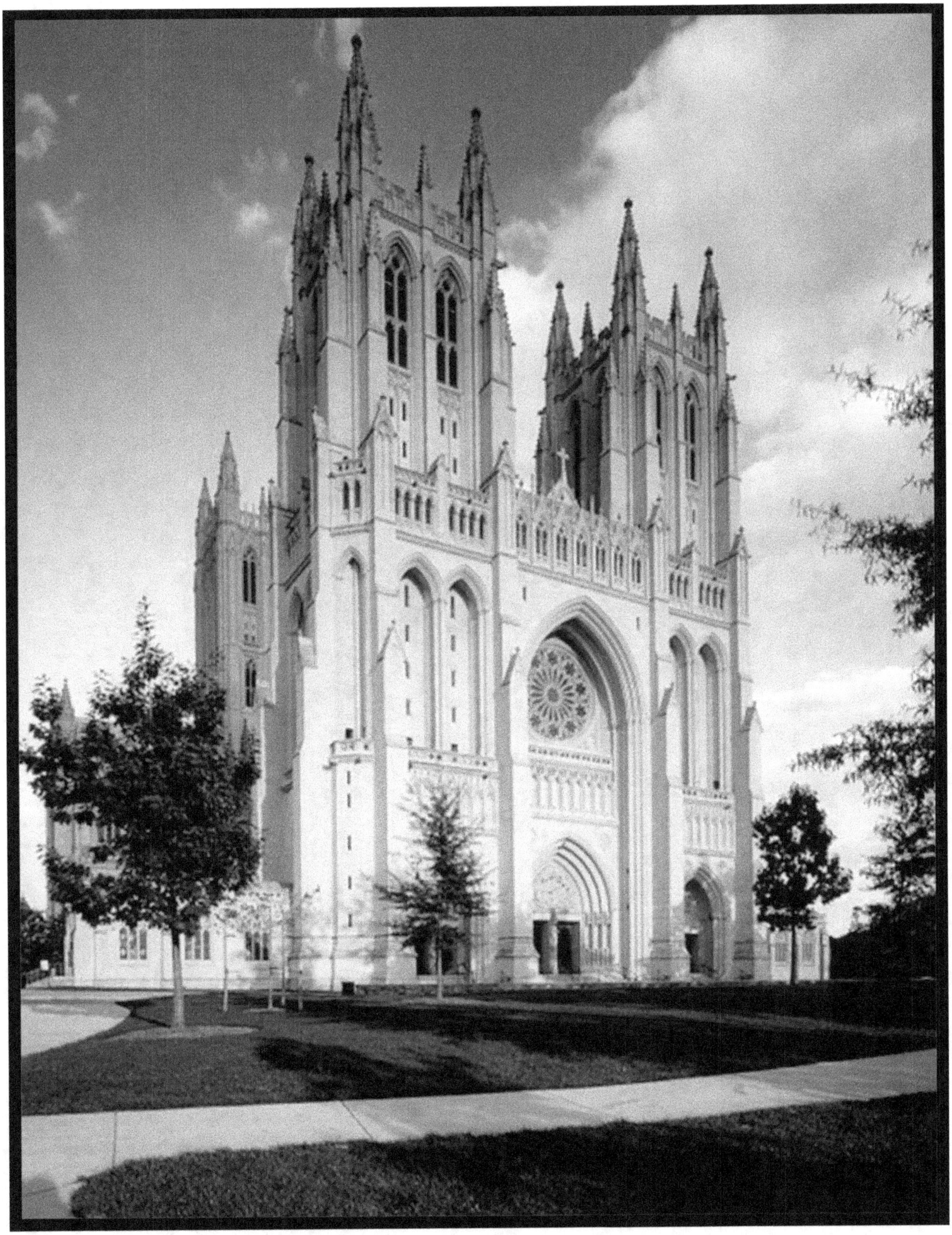

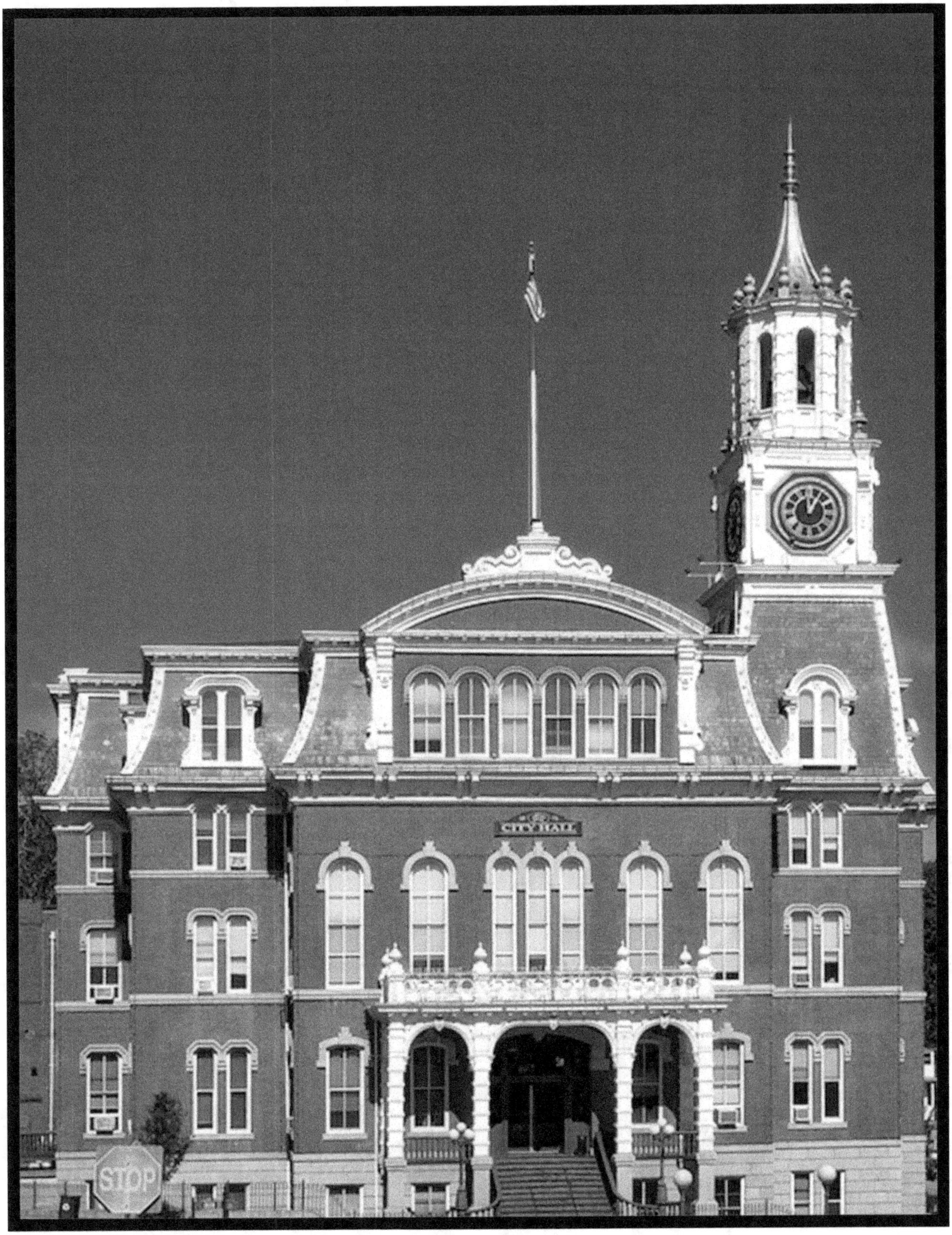
CITY HALL
STOP

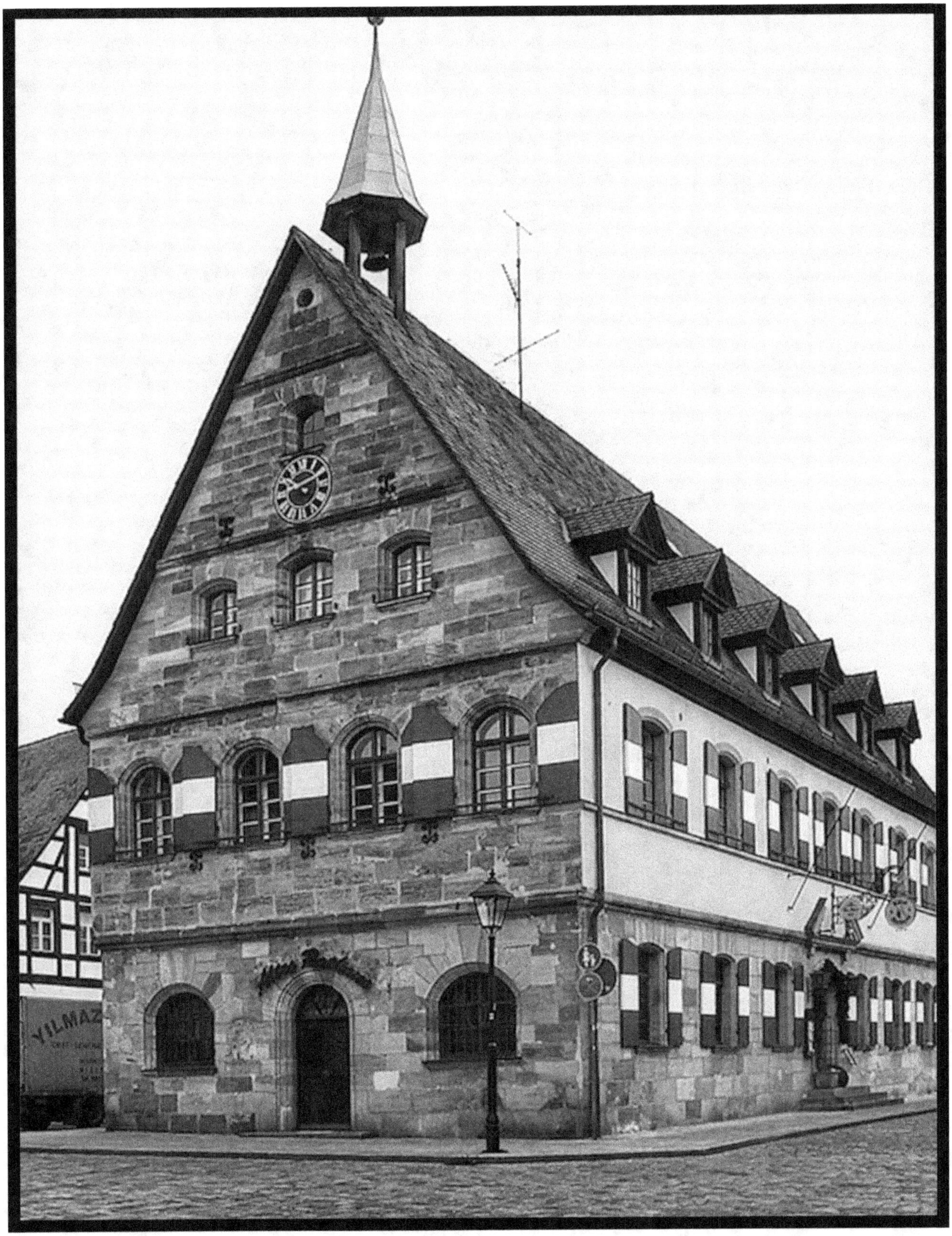
YILMAZ

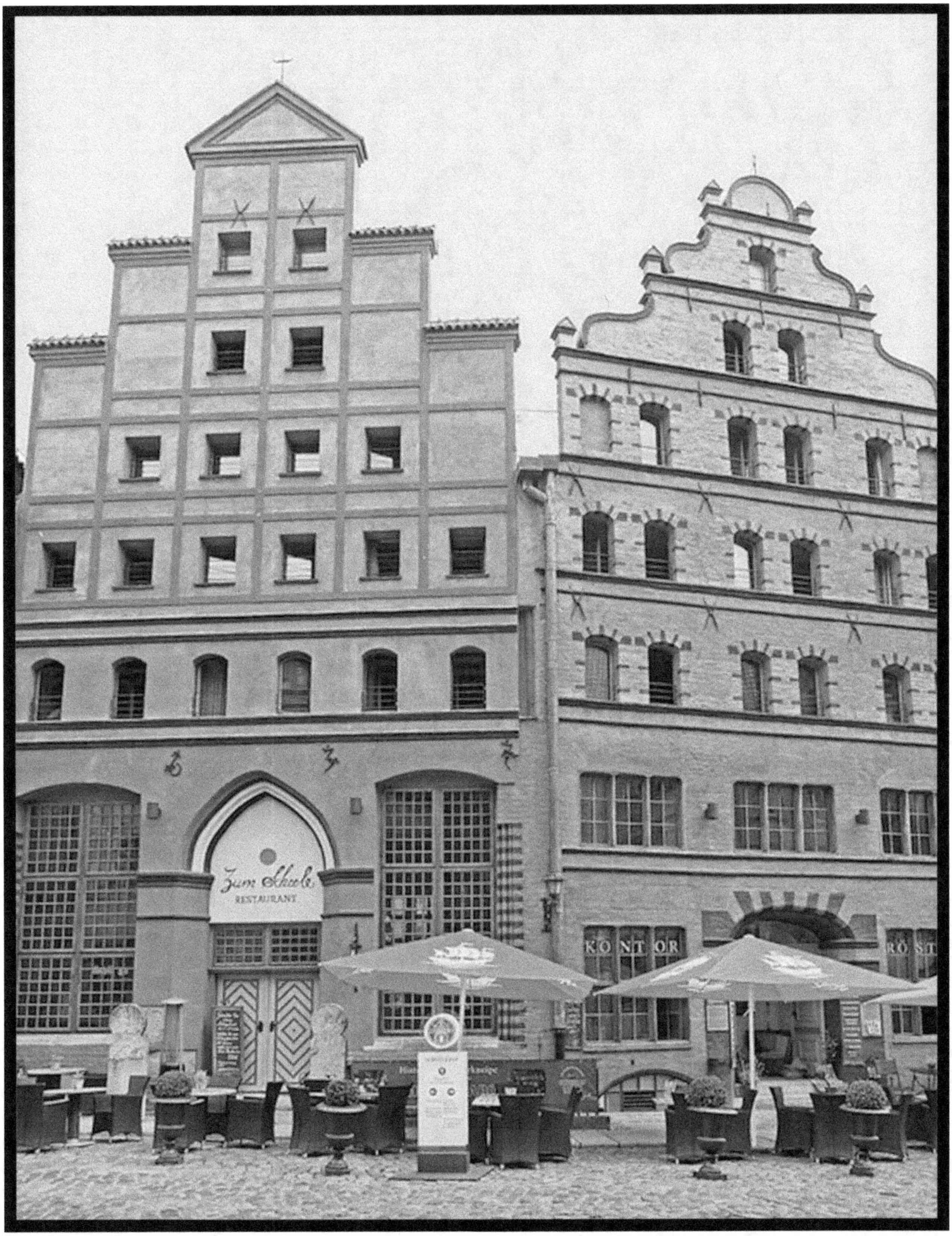
Zum Scheele
RESTAURANT
KONTOR

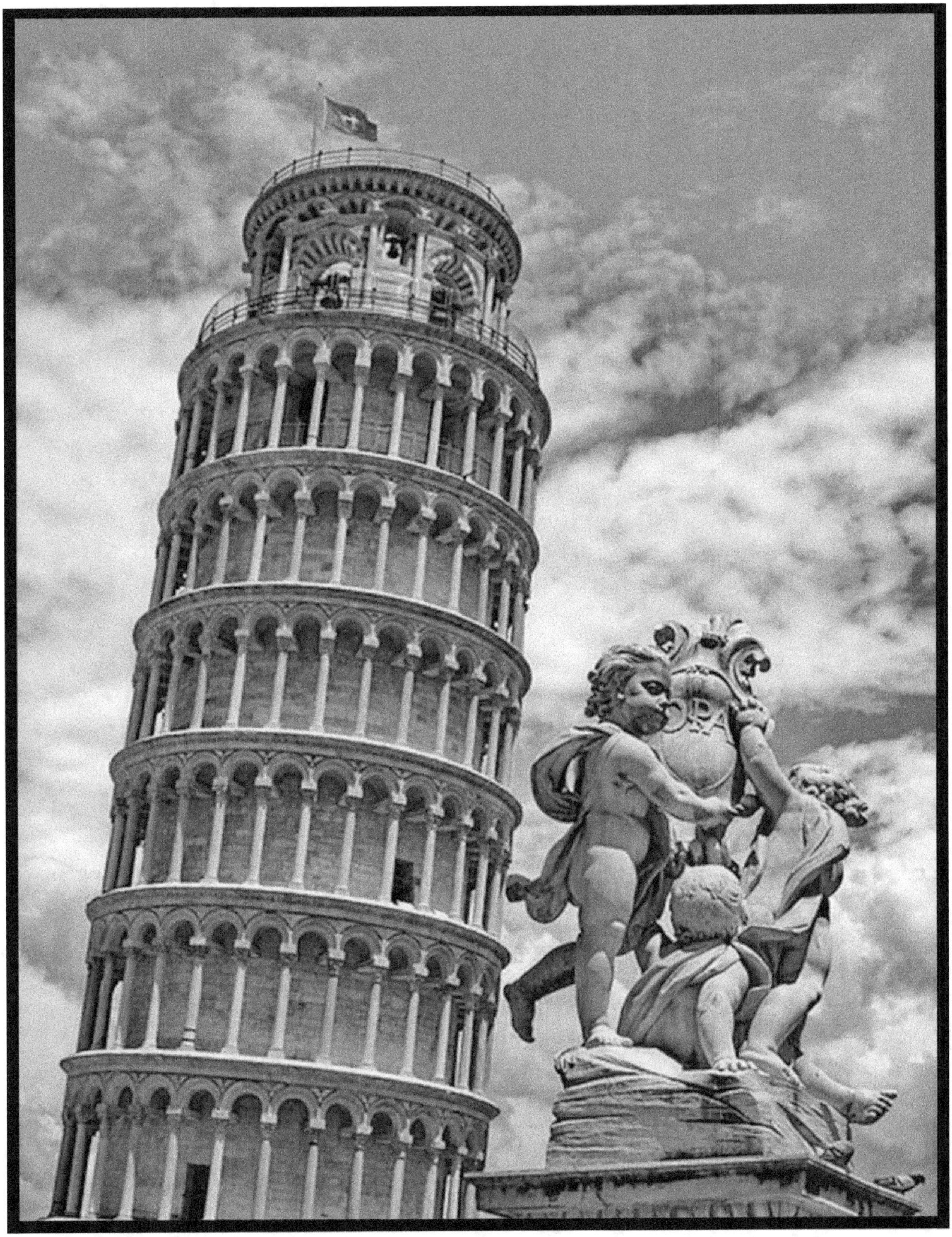

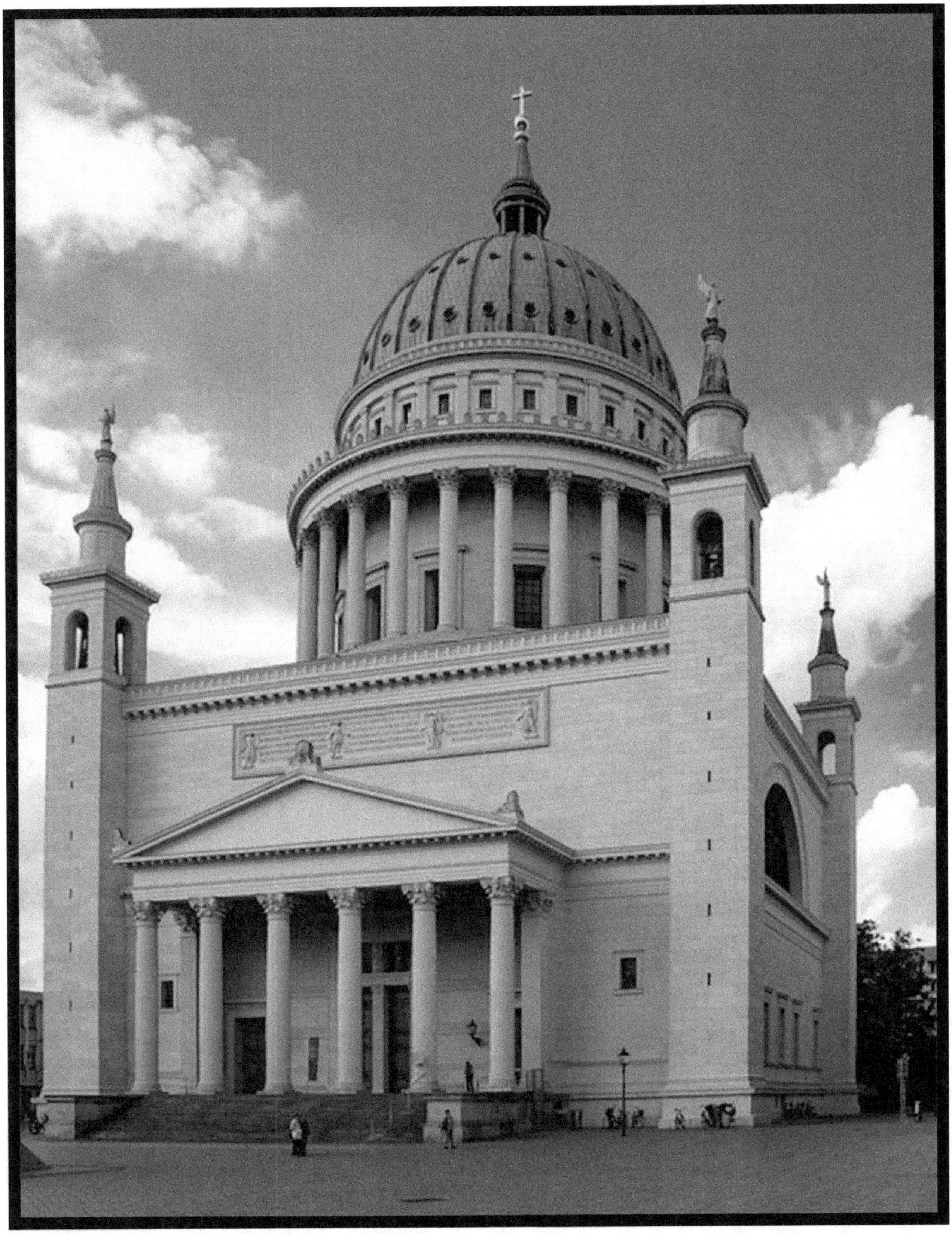

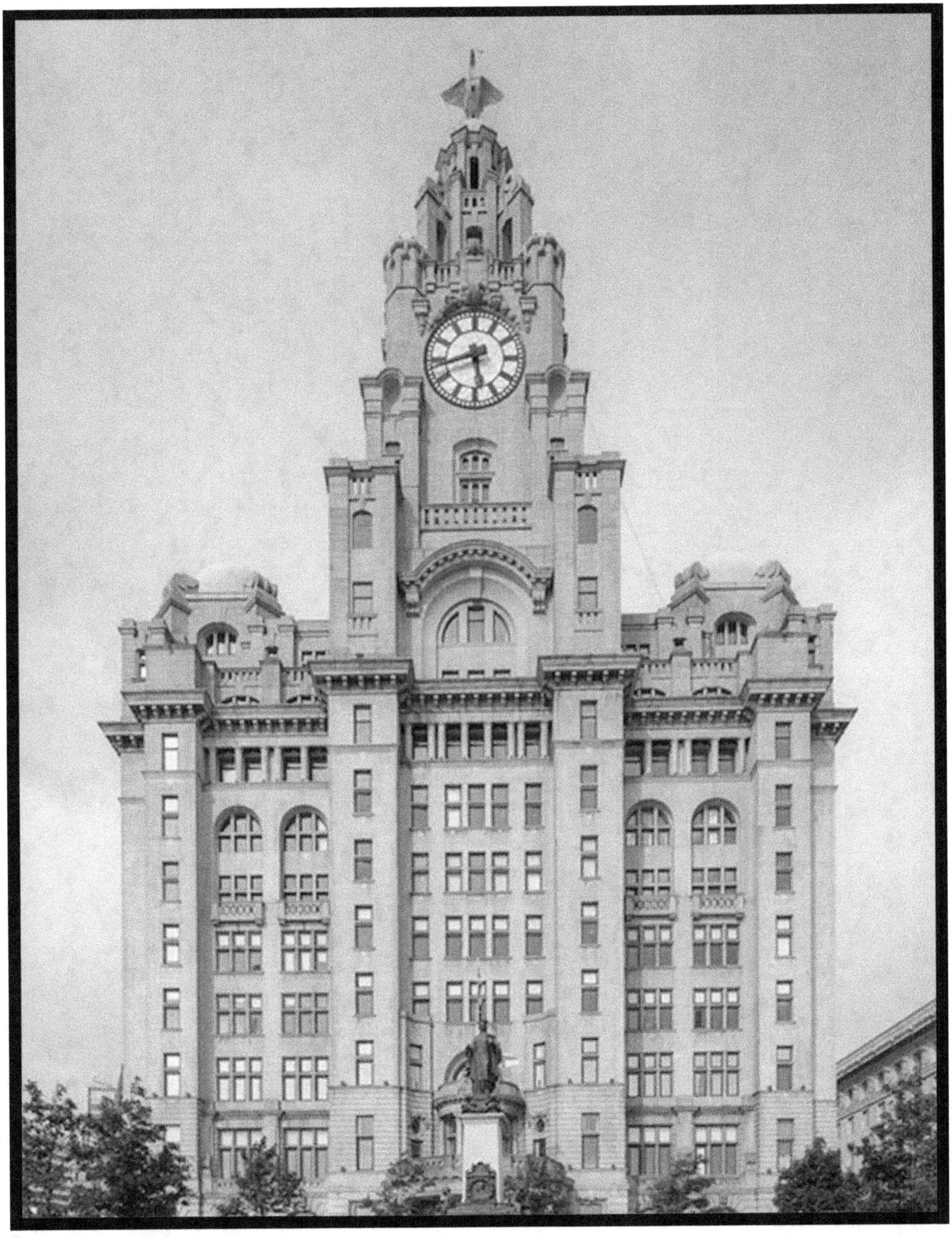

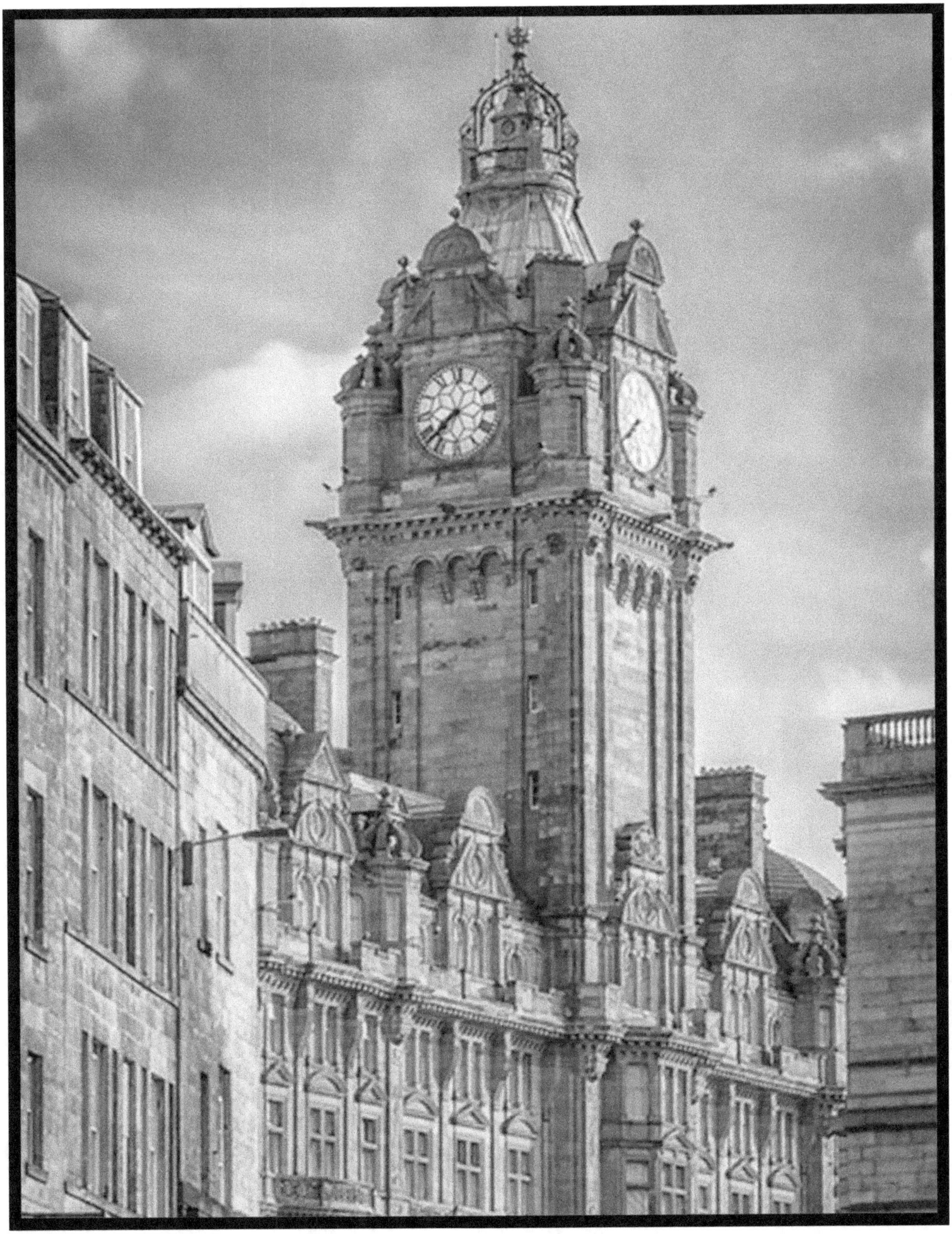

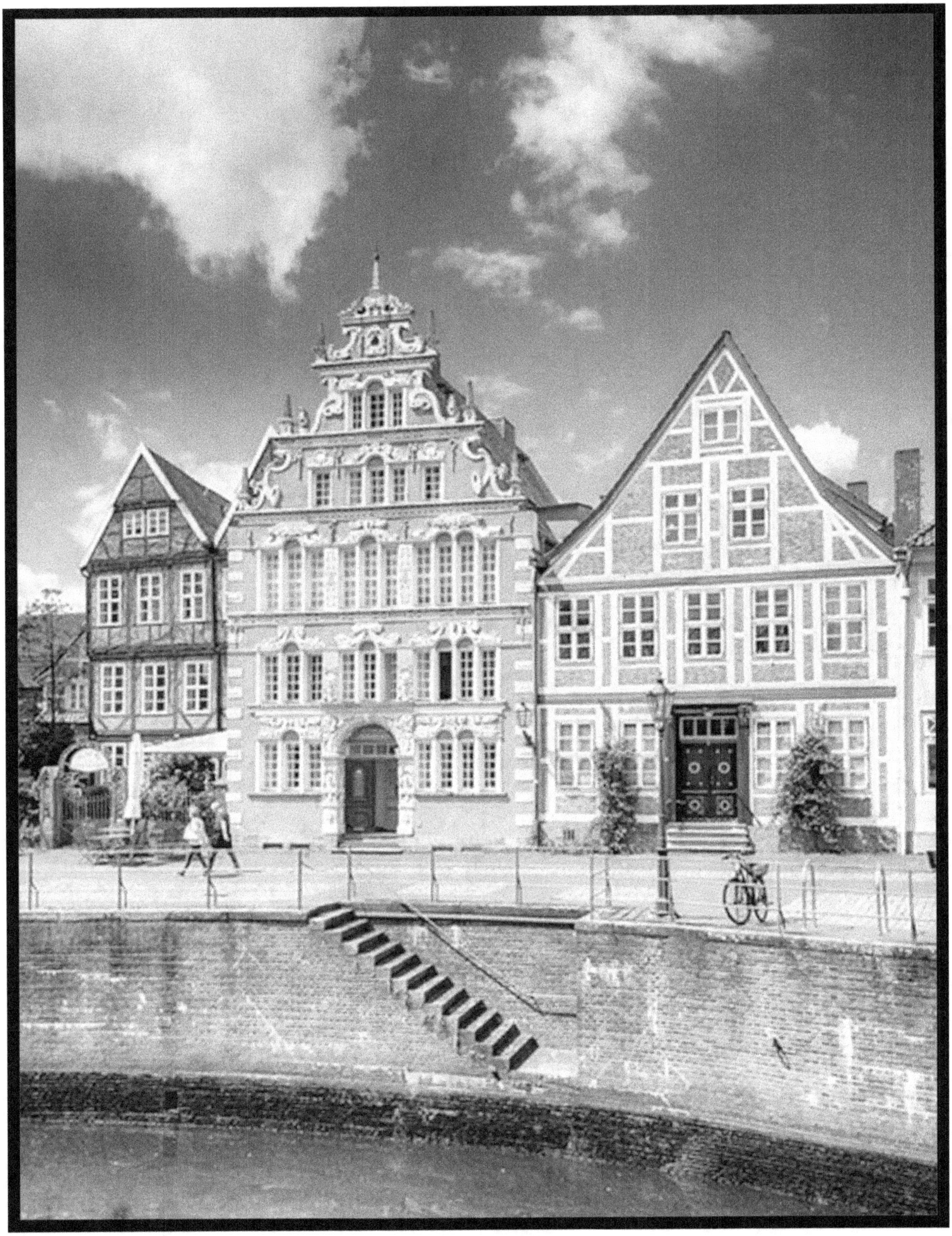

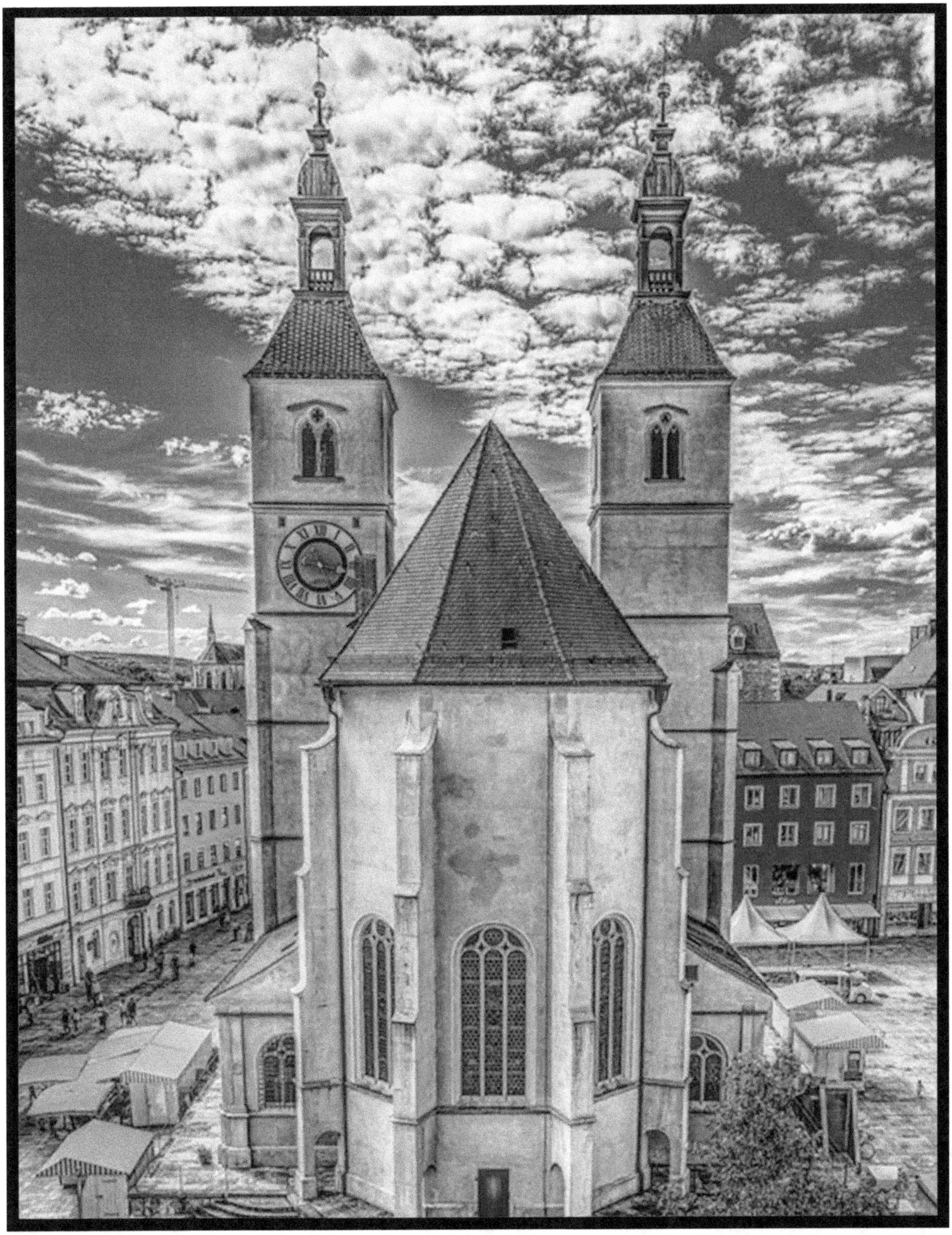

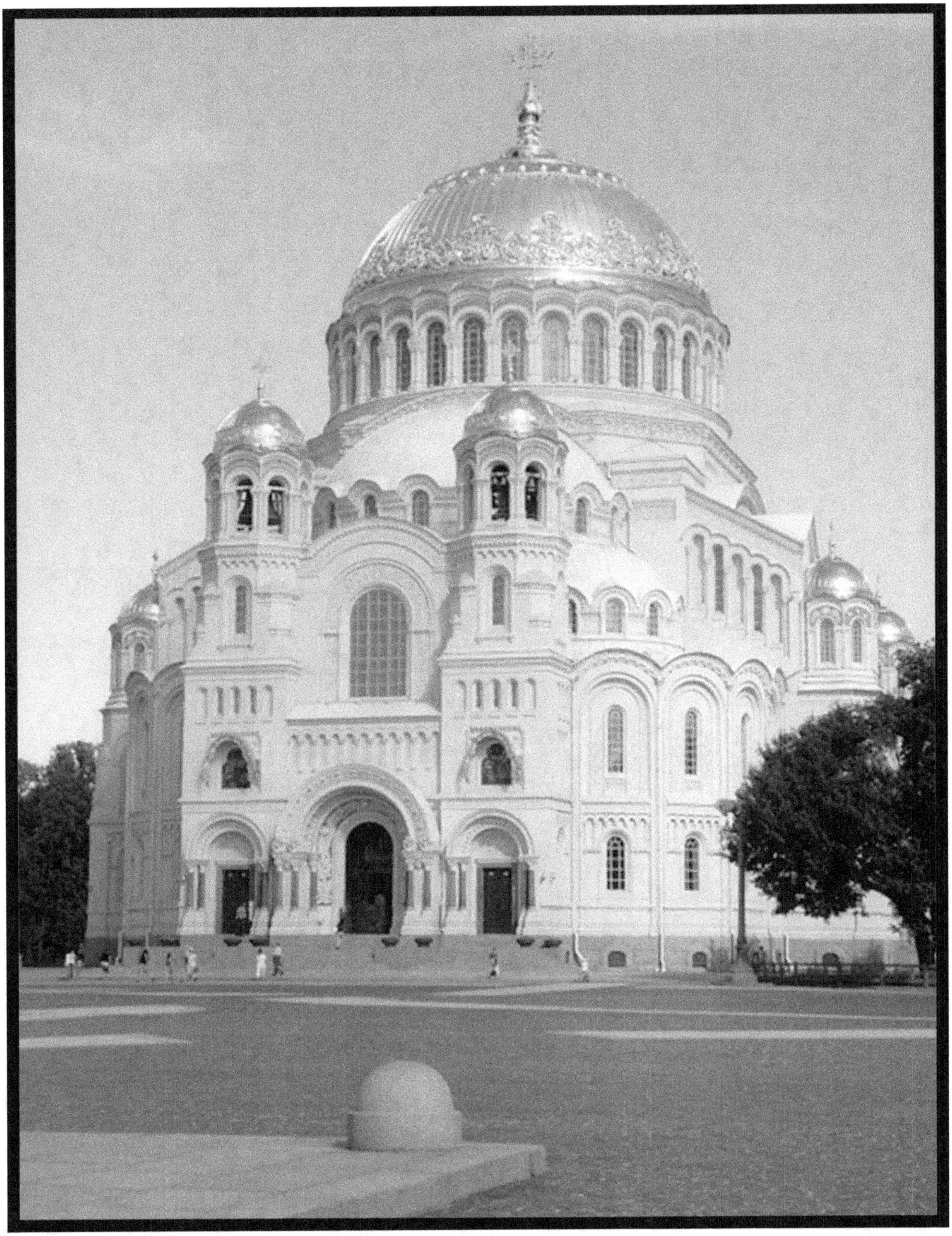

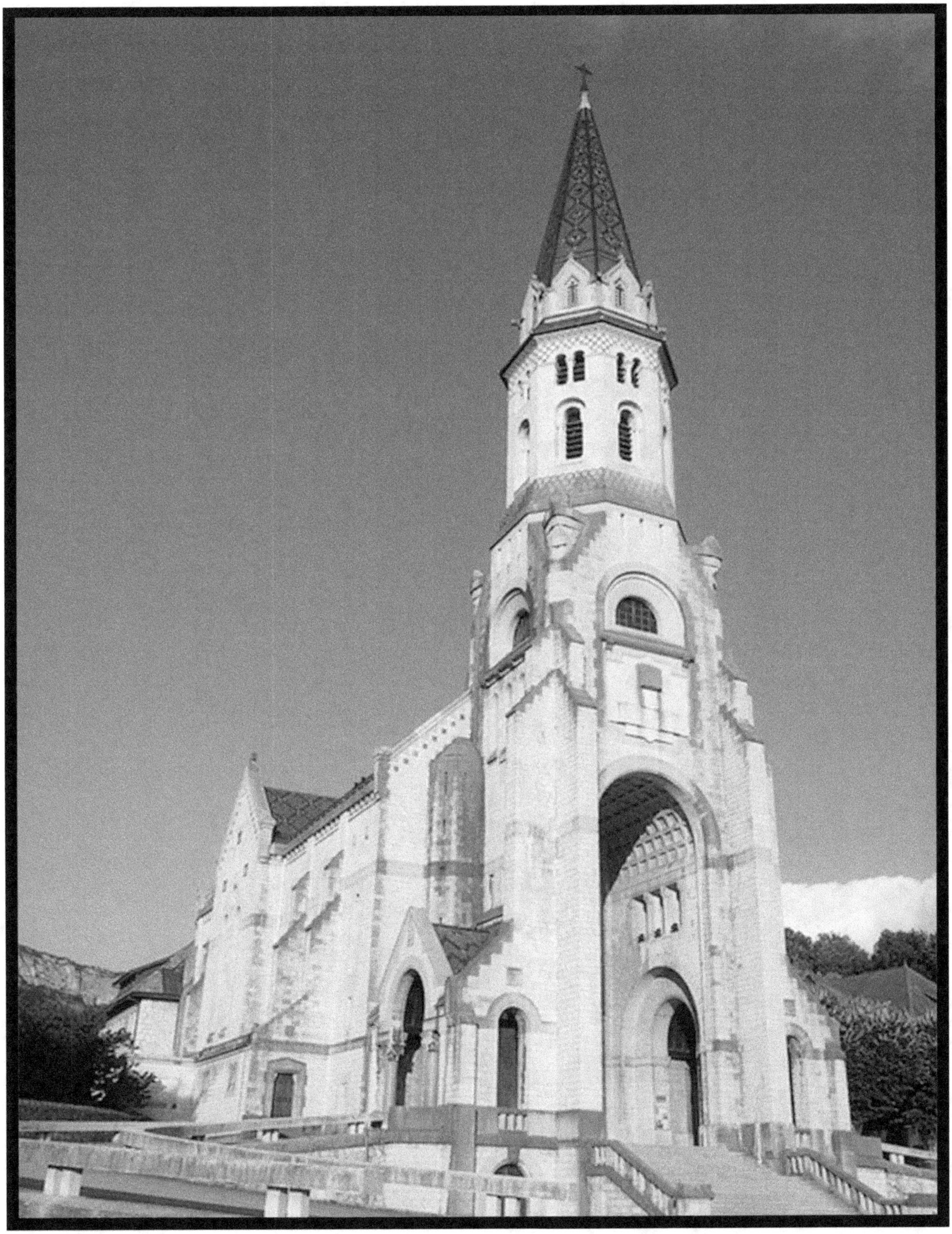

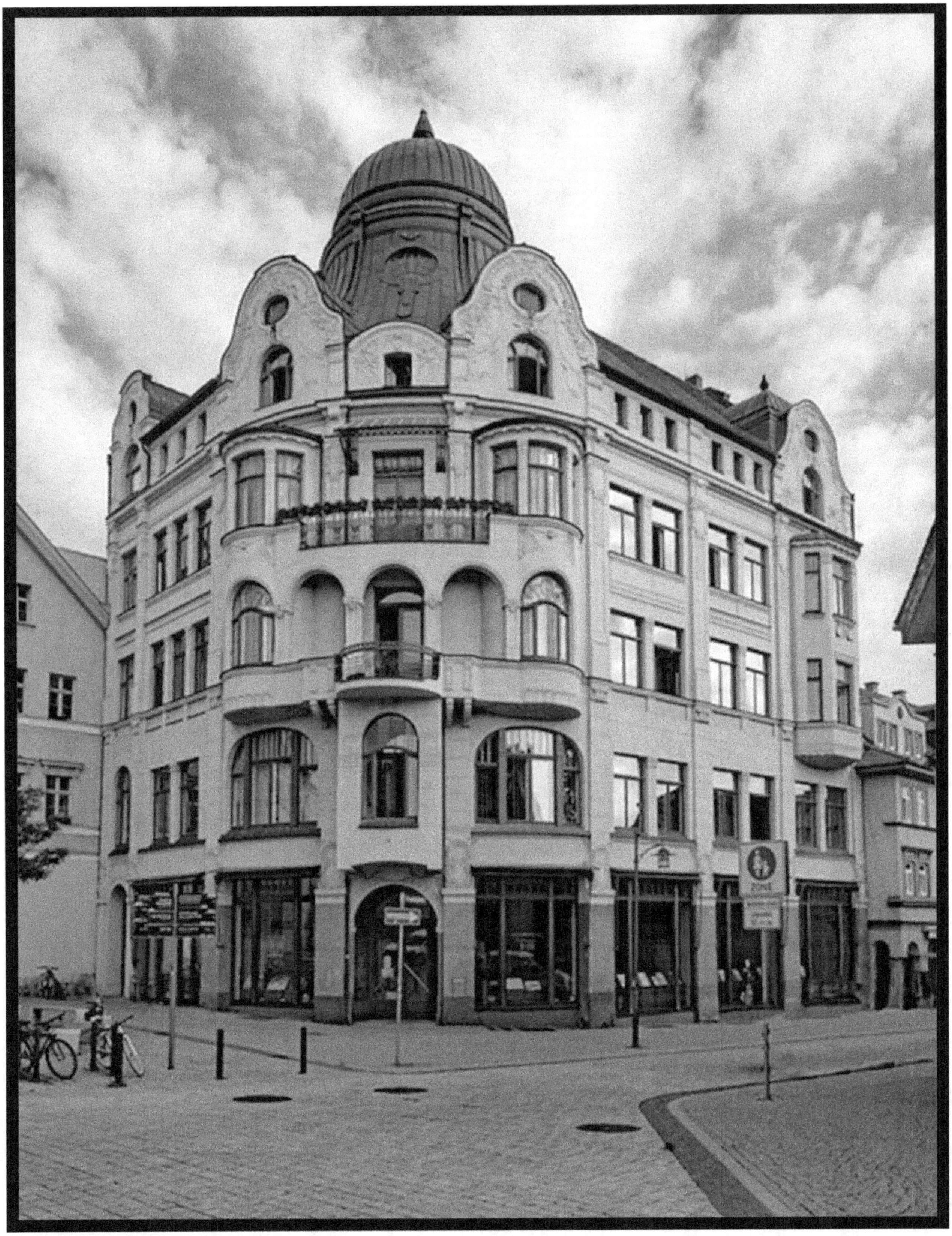

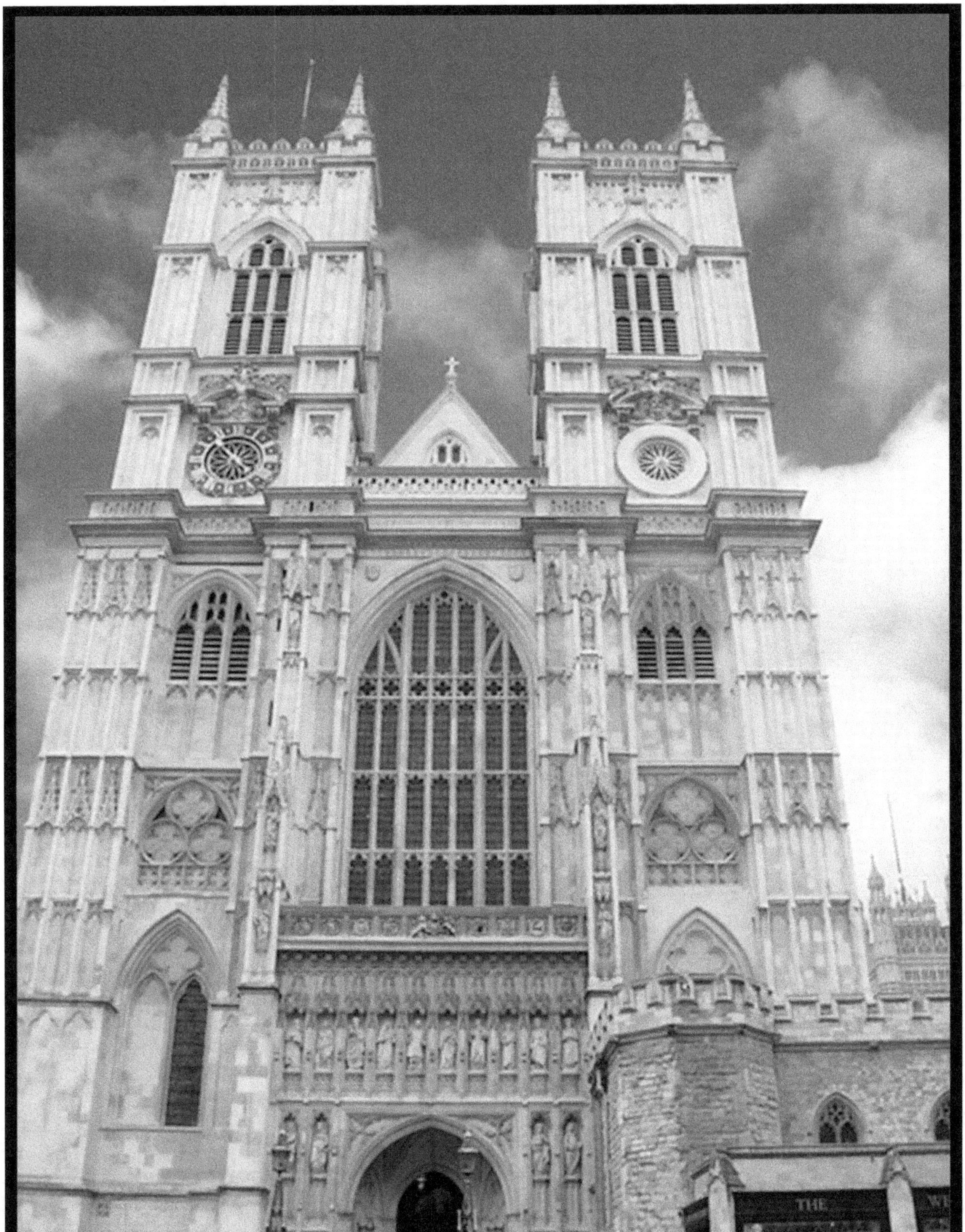
THE

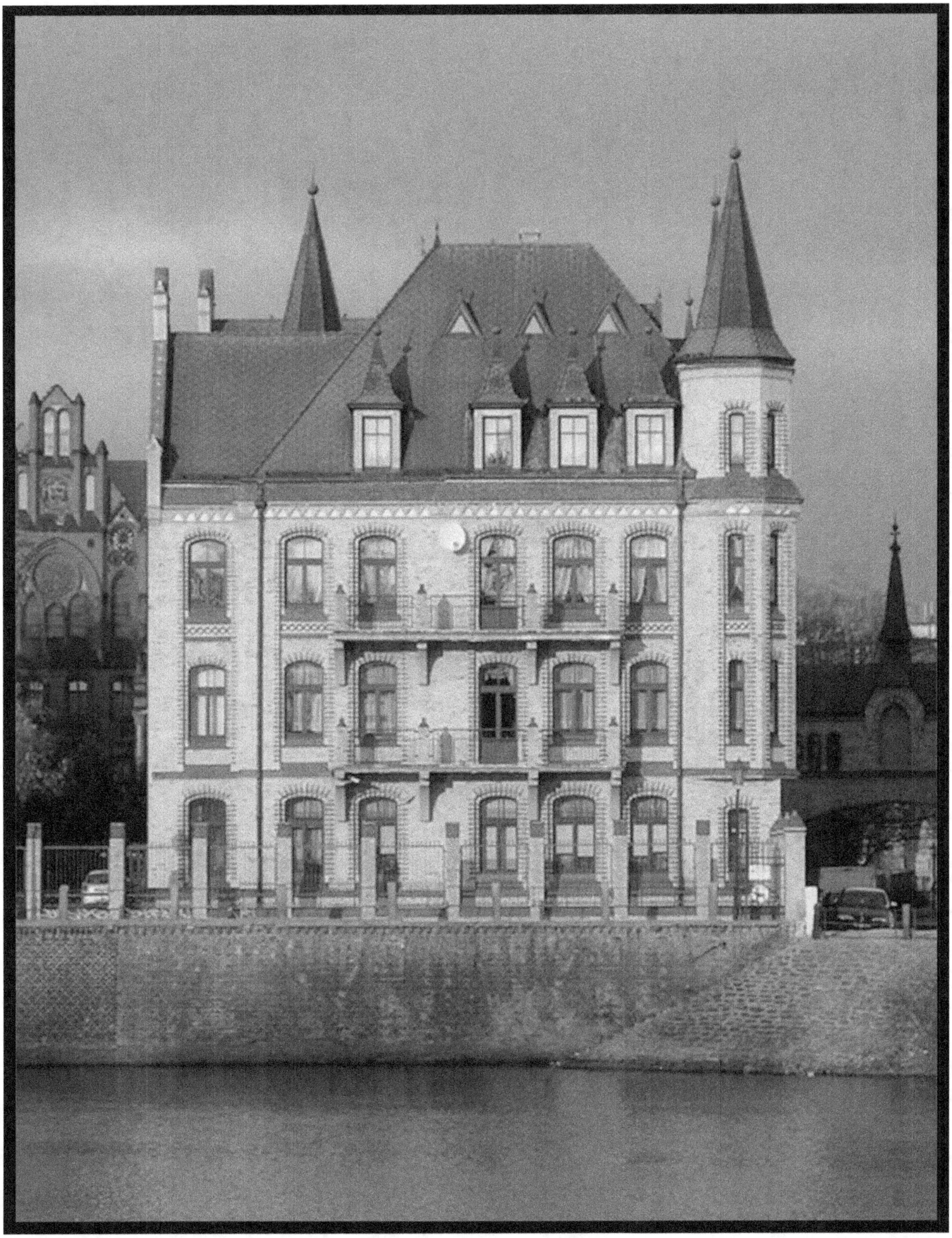

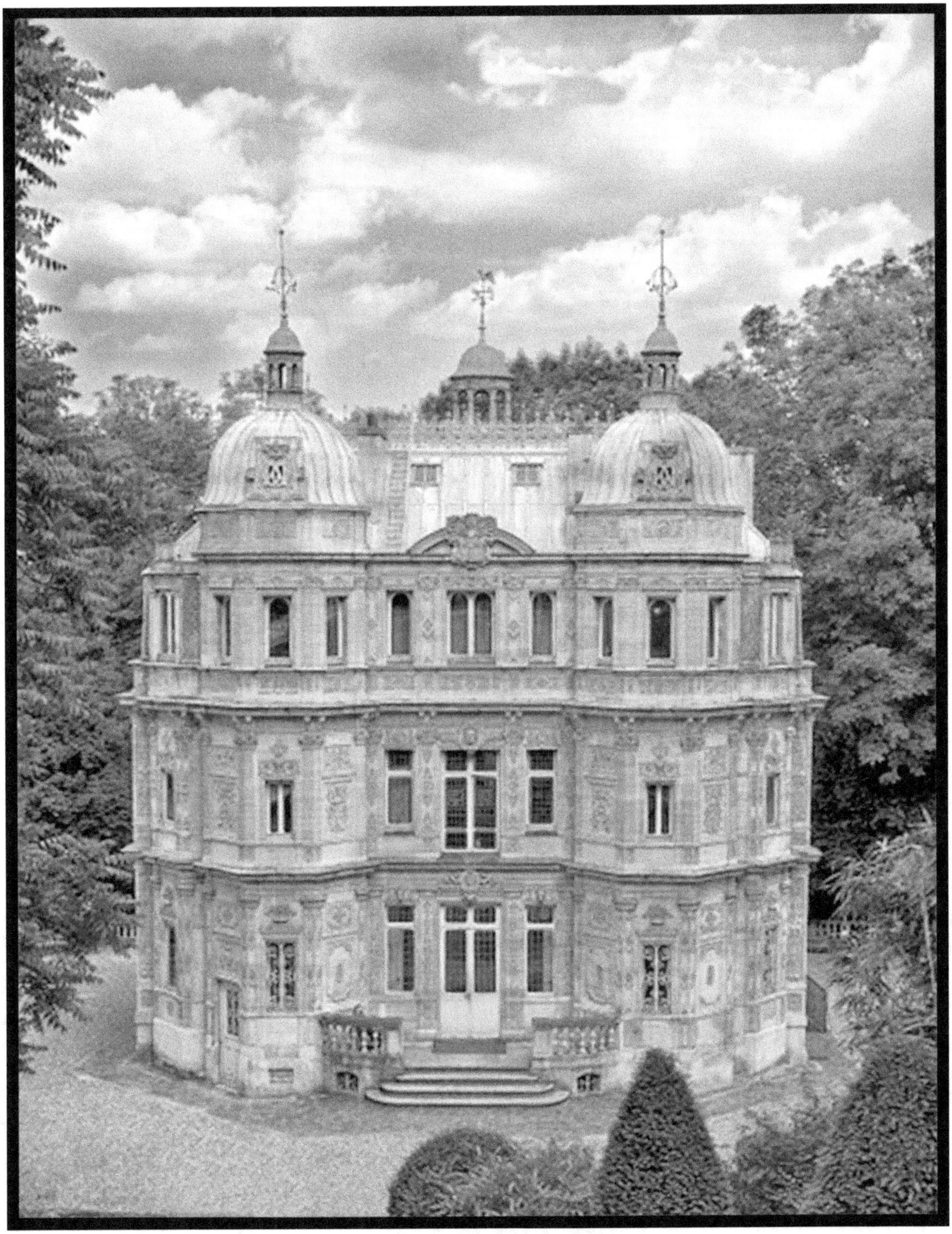

www.ingramcontent.com/pod-product-compliance
Lightning Source LLC
Chambersburg PA
CBHW082008230526
45468CB00023B/2828
* 9 7 8 1 7 2 3 3 9 9 5 6 5 *